Calm

Kim L. Hazelton, OTR/L

Copyright © 2020 Kim L. Hazelton

All rights reserved.

ISBN: 9798642591918

DEDICATION

I dedicate this book to my family, Frank, Luke, and Mo. You are my life.

I further dedicate it to the precious families who have graciously allowed me to enter into their lives and go on a journey of helping, healing, and hope with them. You are my mission.

This book is not intended to be a substitute for professional medical advice, diagnosis, or treatment. Always seek the advice of your physician or other qualified health provider with any questions you may have regarding a medical condition. Never disregard professional medical advice or delay in seeking it because of something you have read in this book. But please use this book as a catalyst and support for dialogue with your medical professional.

CONTENTS

Chapter 1: An Introduction to Fight, Flight, Freeze   1

Chapter 2: How Can I Tell if My Child is Experiencing a Flight, Fight, or Freeze Response?   5

Chapter 3: What a Child Needs to Develop Self-Calming Skills   11

Chapter 4: How to Get the Most Benefit from this Book   24

Chapter 5: Fight, Flight, Freeze Reduction Techniques   29
    Prayer and Meditation   30
    Hydration   32
    Whole Brain Activation   34
    Breath Control   38
    Sensory: Tactile & Proprioception   44
    Sensory: Vestibular   58
    Sensory: Auditory   67
    Sensory: Visual   69
    Sensory: Olfactory (Smell) & Gustatory (Taste)   72
    Sensory: Interoception   74
    Behavioral   78
    Physiological   81
    Alternative   84

Notes: 90

Resources   92

1 An Introduction to Fight, Flight, Freeze

A child who
- gets into fights at school
- becomes aggressive with a sibling
- has tantrums
- screams
- throws things
- breaks things
- runs away
- doesn't listen or follow directions
- refuses to eat certain foods
- won't make eye contact
- shuts down when asked to do something
- won't speak
- cries at the drop of a hat
- can't remember what they just learned
- gets upset at the smallest things, and
- is ostracized by peers

may be experiencing a state of Fight, Flight, or Freeze during these moments. This is a survival reaction in response to something that feels scary or threatening to them. If we take a moment to understand how this happens, we can better help them calm down in the moment, and calm down in general so that this response happens less often.

First we need to understand WHY they are acting this way. All behavior is communication, and we can learn much from our child's behavior if we are willing to listen with our hearts. Undesirable behavior in our children is an S.O.S. signal. We can either rescue them, or we can increase the stress. I've been guilty of both. And I'm going to share what I've learned as a human being, as a parent to two unique, beautiful, weird, intelligent children, and as a Pediatric Occupational Therapist for over 25 years. In fact, the driving reason I've learned all of this is because of my own experiences and the experiences of my children.

You and your child need to have an emotional connection. If things have gotten difficult enough that you've purchased my book, odds are that that emotional connection is strained at best. So the first thing I want you to do is to tell your child that you are on *their* team. That you want them to feel safe, secure, and confident enough to do the things they *like and want* to do, but to also do the things they *have* to do without feeling so bad about any of it. That you know that it doesn't feel good to lose control of your emotions or behavior. That you want to help them feel comfortable in their own skin. That you want to see them succeed at being a kid who can learn and have fun. That you want the rest of the world to know what kind, smart, funny, and caring people they are. That you believe in them.

Then hug them and tell them that you love them.

The key to calming the Fight, Flight, Freeze response is for the child to have a sense of safety and security. Ideally, **you** as the parent(s) *are* that initial safety and security. You provide for all of their needs, and they become confident enough to venture away from you because they know that they can return to you as their soft landing when things become scary or overwhelming. As they venture further from that safe nest you created for them, they will return to it periodically to rest and recharge before going on bigger and bigger adventures. Eventually, they develop and manage their own sense of safety and security internally, utilizing tools they develop as they grow. Tools like the ones you will find in this book.

If you are the person who gets the brunt of their undesirable behavior, consider yourself loved and connected to the child. They will typically let their true emotions of fear, frustration, anger, and humiliation come out with only the most trusted people. If they can count on you to love them even when they are at their worst, they feel safe to show you their worst. You have done a great job instilling a sense of safety for them with you. And by buying this book, you are doing a great job learning more techniques to help them grow into someone who can better control their emotions and behaviors, and successfully navigate the path to good health, solid learning, and loving, mutually supportive relationships in life.

Let's dig in and learn to read their signals better.

2 How Can I Tell if My Child is Experiencing a Flight, Fight, or Freeze Response?

It doesn't always look the way you think it does.

It often comes as a surprise to parents when I tell them that, based upon behavior I can see in my office, their child is in a state of Flight. The child is not running away from anyone. As a matter of fact, they might be excitedly exploring the large Sensory Gym we have in the office. So what would lead me to believe that they are in a state of Flight? It's the *pattern* of exploration in the Sensory Gym.

A child who enters my office in a state of Flight might still experience the excitement of the obvious opportunities to play on the swings and balls and the scooter board and ramp, but rather than explore everything throughout the room, they will explore the items farthest away from me - the *perceived* possible threat. If I slowly move gently around in the Sensory Gym, they will "conveniently" become interested in a play opportunity that is farther away from me than the one they were currently exploring. And if I get too close, or approach their exploratory play too many times, they will retreat to the parent, and often transition into a state of Freeze by hiding behind the parent (often crouched in a ball, or literally squeezing behind them in the chair), avoiding eye contact, refusing to communicate or return to the play opportunities, and disobeying all commands from the parent to re-engage in the evaluation or treatment session.

Let's look at some behavior indicators that will let you know which state of sympathetic distress your child may be experiencing.

Freeze

- Disinterest
- Forgetfulness
- Appearing to be unaware of what's expected of them
- Unable to start a task
- Unable to progress through a task - just sits there and stares
- Daydreaming
- Appears to be trying not to be noticed
- Appears to be trying to be "small"

Flight

- Running away
- Staying active or busy (in an effort to avoid the *perceived* threatening task)
- Rarely has free time to just be
- Impulsive/jittery
- Baby talks, makes silly sounds, communicates immaturely
- Acts immaturely silly, class clown
- Maintains distance (from *perceived* threat)
- Is extremely competitive and has a drive to always be first or the best.
- Can be controlling

Fight

- Angry
- Aggressive, physically, verbally and/or emotionally
- Argumentative
- Blames others
- Contradicts authority
- Boastful
- Needs to control
- Lies, sometimes for no apparent gain
- Self-isolating
- Self-imposed rules keeper

Let's look at some scenarios to help you understand how a child might look disobedient, but is in reality experiencing acute distress.

1. Let's revisit the scenario I briefly described above. E was a 4-year-old little boy who had been brought to my office for an evaluation due to his parents concerns regarding his aggressive behaviors toward his little brother. His parents reported that they are loving, but stern parents, and do not tolerate this kind of behavior. At his initial appointment, he looked like a happy little boy who was excited to come in and play in the Big Sensory Gym. While Mom and I sat on one side of the room and I gathered information from her, E explored the gym, but only the items on the side of the gym farthest from where Mom and I were sitting. I invited Mom to join me as we walked toward E, still having a calm conversation. E noticed us coming nearer and "happily" walked the perimeter of the gym to another play spot that was farthest from where I was with Mom. I quietly asked Mom to walk over to E and ask him about what he was exploring, and she did. He remained at that location with her until I started to slowly walk over while talking gently to Mom, at which point he "happily" walked the perimeter of the room to another play spot that was farthest away from me. E was obviously in flight from his perceived threat - me. E had been experiencing acute distress, and he appeared to be transitioning most often between flight and fight. Once I explained what this behavior represented, the parents reported that he often did this at home as well, and they just thought he was being disobedient so they disciplined him. E likely knew enough not to take out his Fight response on his parents, so his little brother became an easy target.

2. B was a 5-year-old boy brought to my office for an evaluation due to him getting in trouble at school and falling behind in academics. From a very young age, he had seen his mother abused by his father, and he had experienced abuse at the hands of his father as well. The parents were now divorced, and Mom and B were now living with his grandparents in a new state. When B initially came in for the evaluation, he sat in the chair in the corner farthest from the office

door, head down, shoulders rounded forward, and his long, curly hair almost completely covered his face. He let Mom do most of the talking, and he spoke softly when he did speak. When it was time to enter the Sensory Gym for the evaluation, B did so, but kept his arms and legs close to his body, and when I asked him to sit on the floor mat, he assumed a "crouched" position instead. B was in a state of Freeze, but on the verge of Flight (crouched instead of sitting) if the need arose.

3. M was an 8-year-old girl brought to my office for an evaluation due to both parents' concern regarding her recent physical violence toward her twin sister. They reported that she's always been a straight A student and got along with peers at school, but that she's always had a disagreeable nature. If they said their red car was red, she would insist that it wasn't truly red, but was maroon. If they said it was sunny outside, she'd respond that it was partly cloudy. They reported that it was impossible to please M, even if you gave her exactly what she asked for. She would burst into fits of rage or tears at the drop of a hat, and the whole family walked on eggshells not knowing what would set her off next. It appeared that M was indeed struggling with something, and was keeping it together during the day at school, but released her Fight response at home on those who she loved and trusted the most, particularly her twin sister.

4. M was an 11-year-old girl brought to my office for an evaluation due to struggling in school. M consistently got good grades, but she spent 4-6 hours a night on homework *after* participating in 1-2 hours worth of extra-curriculars after school. And she suffered frequent headaches. She had recently been to a Developmental Optometrist and was wearing the glasses he prescribed, but that didn't seem to help with the headaches. Mom was concerned that M would fall behind academically and do poorly on the PSAT, SAT, and ACT once she got to high school, in 3 years. At the initial appointment, M sat next to her Mom, nearly on her lap. She was wearing baggy

sweatpants and an oversized, baggy hoodie with the hood up over her head and her long hair partially covering her face. M refused to leave Mom's side during the initial interview, or during the follow-up appointment to attempt to evaluate her. M was in a state of Freeze.

5. Finally, K was a 30-something year old woman with a husband in the military and two young children. K's husband was gone frequently on deployments and training, often for up to 9 months out of each year. K was left to raise their two unique children with limited support from her husband, and none from extended family. She was also working a full-time job, taking care of a house, and volunteering in their church. K spent most days in a state of Fight, but was unaware of it. She thought she was just an aggressive problem solver. K's breaking point came when their garage freezer broke for the 5th time in as many months, and despite the fact that it was still under warranty, the company refused to repair it again, or replace it. K. angrily jumped on the back of the repair van as it pulled out of her driveway, and she rode it out of their residential neighborhood while her two precious preschool-aged children napped in their bedrooms and while K's husband was fighting a war in a foreign country. K was in an extreme acute Fight response. I am K, and this did happen to me. And that was my catalyst to finding calming techniques so that I could better handle my stress. Life is full of stressors. They never stop coming. We would all do well to learn how to better manage the emotions and behaviors that those stressors trigger.

And if that Sears repairman ever reads this book, I want him to know how sorry I am that I scared him like that.

3 What a Child Needs to Develop Self-Calming Skills

Maslow's Hierarchy of Needs and the Autonomic Nervous System

We're going to take a brief look at what goes on inside our child's body to cause them to have a fight, flight, or freeze response to something. First, let's look at what psychologist Abraham Maslow theorized in 1943 in his paper "A Theory of Human Motivation".

Maslow's Hierarchy of Needs

According to Maslow's hierarchy of needs, we humans are designed to seek to survive before any other need. The first thing we require to be able to grow, progress, and develop skills and knowledge are basic life sustaining items such as food and shelter.

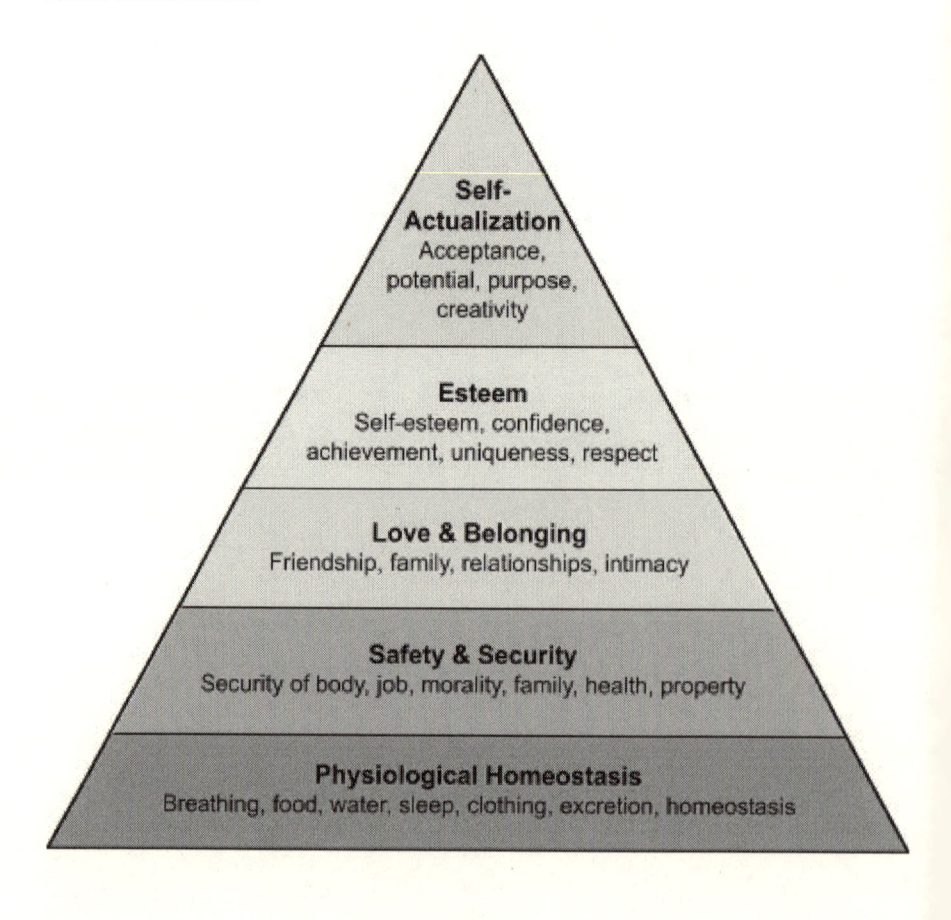

Self-Actualization
Acceptance, potential, purpose, creativity

Esteem
Self-esteem, confidence, achievement, uniqueness, respect

Love & Belonging
Friendship, family, relationships, intimacy

Safety & Security
Security of body, job, morality, family, health, property

Physiological Homeostasis
Breathing, food, water, sleep, clothing, excretion, homeostasis

The critically important concept here is that it is the individual's *perception or feeling* of needs being met that matters.

Think of something that creates a sense of fear/anxiety for you, such as riding roller coasters. It is likely that no amount of assurance from loved ones or amusement park personnel regarding the safety statistics of riding that roller coaster will convince your body to turn down the stress response and strap in to that seat! You don't *feel* a sense of **Safety & Security** regarding getting onto that ride.

Why does this matter and what does this mean for our children?

It doesn't matter if **you** know that your child is safe if **they** don't **perceive/feel** that they are safe.

It doesn't matter if **you** know that broccoli is safe and good for your child if **their** brain is **perceiving** that that stiff, crunchy, mixed-texture, green item is NOT safe for them to put into their mouth.

Returning to Maslow's hierarchy of needs, we need to recognize that we shift up and down through these needs throughout our lives; often throughout our day. In every situation and environment, once we *feel* that our physiological needs have been met, we then seek to *feel* safe and secure and so on, moving up the pyramid as high as we can within that particular situation and environment.

Example: Imagine that you are having dinner with friends in a lovely restaurant in a delightful part of town and the weather is beautiful. The meal is over and you and your friends are enjoying sharing stories and laughing together. Your needs at the **Physiological** level, **Safety & Security** level, **Love & Belonging** level, and the **Esteem** level are being met beautifully. Your Fight, Flight, Freeze response is practically turned off and you are blissfully chill and happy. Then you hear a loud noise from the kitchen and start to smell smoke! Your brain immediately shifts back down to the **Safety**

& Security level of need and your sense of smell, hearing, and vision become heightened, disregarding the conversation you were just having with your friends. (Don't worry, your friends' brains are going through the same shift so they're disregarding the conversation as well and don't perceive you as rude.) The restaurant manager comes out and apologizes for the commotion and assures everyone that there is no danger, and your brain shifts out of **Safety & Security** and back up to **Love & Belonging**, smiling and rejoicing with your friends how grateful you are that you are all safe. Pretty cool how our brains shift up and down like that, huh?

Now, imagine your child in school and for whatever reason, they do not *feel* safe and secure. The majority of their energy will be spent seeking **Safety & Security**, limiting the amount of energy they can spend on paying attention, following directions, socializing, and learning.

Acute Stress Response

Leaving Maslow's Hierarchy of Needs now, let's look at how our body responds to stress/threat (real and not-really-real-but-perceived-but-the-brain-doesn't-know-the-difference).

At this point it would be helpful to understand the basic makeup of our nervous system. The human nervous system consists of two main parts, the Central Nervous System (CNS) and the Peripheral Nervous System (PNS). The PNS is further divided into two main parts, the Somatic Nervous System and the Autonomic Nervous System. And the Autonomic Nervous System is then divided into two more parts: The Parasympathetic Nervous System (PNS) and the Sympathetic Nervous System (SNS) which controls our stress response, or our flight, fight, freeze response.

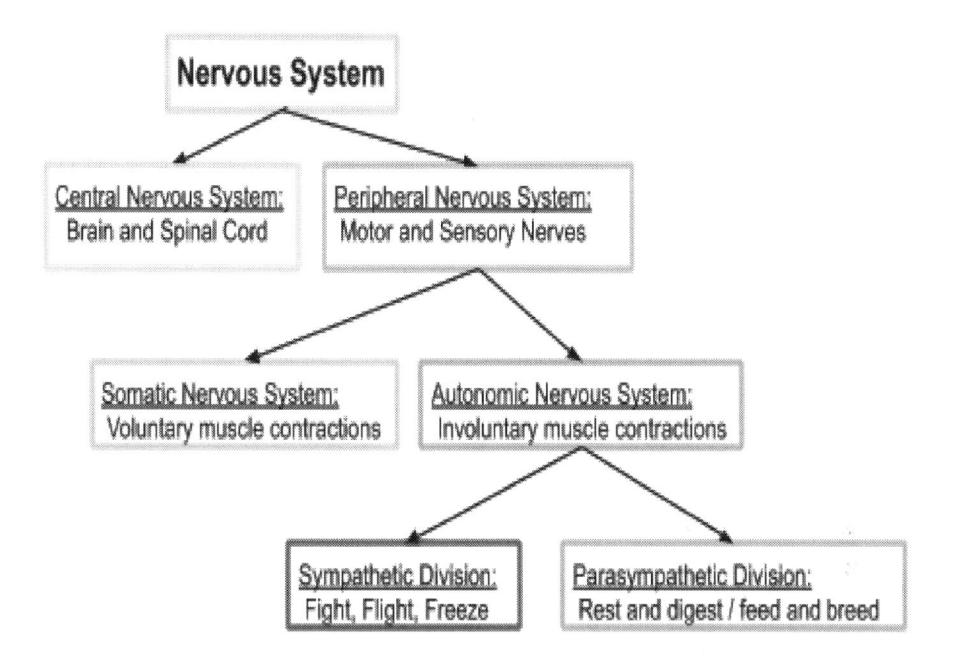

```
Nervous System
├── Central Nervous System:
│   Brain and Spinal Cord
└── Peripheral Nervous System:
    Motor and Sensory Nerves
    ├── Somatic Nervous System:
    │   Voluntary muscle contractions
    └── Autonomic Nervous System:
        Involuntary muscle contractions
        ├── Sympathetic Division:
        │   Fight, Flight, Freeze
        └── Parasympathetic Division:
            Rest and digest / feed and breed
```

First, the body releases hormones to turn the Parasympathetic Nervous System waayyyyy down. That's the part of our nervous system that we like to call the "Feed and Breed" or "Rest and Digest" part. It's a calming and regulating system.

Those hormones also turn the Sympathetic Nervous System waayyyyy up. And that's the part that triggers a Fight, Flight, or Freeze response.

So, what happens when our Sympathetic Nervous System gets turned up?

- Increased heart rate
- Increased blood pressure
- Increased respiration (breathing speed)
- Shallow respiration
- Increased blood clotting factor
- Decreased immune system function
- Decreased stomach/intestinal motility (movement)

- Decreased tear and saliva production
- Decreased overall hearing to enable "Auditory exclusion" so that novel/unfamiliar sounds get greater attention. (Sorry Mom and Dad, your voices are not novel, and they WILL tune you out, only because their Sympathetic Nervous System is forcing them to.)
- Decreased peripheral vision; creates tunnel vision (Mom and Dad, not only can't they "hear" you, they also might not "see" you.)
- Dilation of pupils
- Constriction of blood vessels in organs and dilation of blood vessels in muscles
- Relaxing of bladder
- Disinhibition of spinal reflexes. (This means that their spinal reflexes are allowed to react. This causes a condition called Tendon Guard Reflex/Response. This gets their muscles ready to crouch and tense up to freeze, to spring into action to flee, and/or to posture to fight.)
- Shaking/shivering
- Leg bouncing/shaking

If we use our reasoning skills to understand what this looks like in our child, we can see that it would contribute to:

- Seeking a high sugar and carb diet, to fuel that increased heart rate and respiration, with the resultant sugar highs and crashes and all of the emotional and behavioral challenges that come with that rollercoaster.
- Chronic allergies and illnesses due to decreased immune system function.
- Constipation from a poor diet and lack of digestive motility.
- Leaky gut due to the poor diet and lack of digestive motility.
- "Airy" voice output from the lack of a full, diaphragmatic breath due to the rapid, shallow breathing.
- Dry eyes from decreased tear production affecting vision and perception. Rubbing of eyes.

- Dry mouth from decreased saliva production affecting dental health and possibly speech.
- Poor receptive language skills and direction-following due to "Auditory Exclusion"
- Hyper-attentive to novel noises in the environment - can't tune out novel sounds due to "Auditory Exclusion", but automatically tunes out familiar and safe sounds such as Mom and Dad's voices. Looks very much like Attention Deficit.
- Poor Visual-Perceptual skills from the "Tunnel Vision".
    - May miss objects in their environment and run into things, including walls.
    - Reading challenges, including losing which line they were on when they jump back to the left margin.
    - Handwriting challenges, particularly with reaching the left and right margin.
- Light sensitivity from pupil dilation, possibly contributing to Irlen Syndrome.
- Poor bladder control
- Limited mobility from chronic Tendon Guard Reflex/Response contributes to
    - Toe walking
    - Lower spine and pelvic immobility
    - Shoulder rounding
    - A tendency to fist the hands rather than open. Limited finger isolation and differentiation of sides of the hand, all contributing to handwriting challenges.
- Poor fine motor skills from underlying shaking/tremors and chronic Tendon Guard Reflex.
- Limited social and emotional skills.

Now imagine that this is how your precious 6-year-old little boy feels every day in first grade. Or this is how your 15-year-old daughter feels every time she goes to Youth Group at church. If you're tearing up, go ahead. It's a valid response. Your sweet child is struggling. But there IS something you can do. And the sooner the better.

So what typically happens?

[I'm going to take a time out here to state that there are many factors that can contribute to a child's emotional state. One strong contributor is the presence of active immature reflexes that should have integrated into more mature responses to stimuli, but for some reason have not yet. Two of these reflexes are largely responsible for maintaining a state of increased anxiety and hyper-vigilance: **Fear Paralysis Reflex** and **Moro Reflex**. We are seeing increasing numbers of children in our office that have one or both of these reflexes still active beyond the 3-4 months of age when they should have been integrated. I highly recommend that you look into these two reflexes if your child struggles with controlling their fight, flight, freeze response. The techniques in this book can still help calm your child, but will not entirely eliminate the increased anxiety and stress that these reflexes will cause. A reflex-trained Occupational Therapist can help you determine if these reflexes are still active in your child, and can help get them integrated.]

Dr. Stephen Porges, the originator of the "Poly-vagal Theory" states that our brains make split-second decisions as to which response we will engage in when presented with a perceived threat: either Fight, Flight, or Freeze. And our brains use past experiences to help make that split-second decision.

Below is an example to show how we, as parents, *unintentionally and unknowingly* contribute to the escalation of the Sympathetic Nervous System's Fight, Flight, Freeze response:

1. FREEZE: Our child's first threat response happens in-utero. It's a very useful little reflex called Fear Paralysis. Its sole purpose is self-preservation and it starts (according to some resources) as early as conception - before we even have a brain and spinal cord. So it's a cellular level response. In other words, the embryo wants to live,

and strives to live. What happens is that the embryo, and later fetus, senses a threat primarily through Mom's hormones, and in an effort to conserve Mom's energy resources and to decrease the absorption of possibly harmful substances, the tiny little baby "freezes" until the threat has passed. So, a human's first response to threat (real or **perceived**) is to freeze.

But consider what we do when we tell our child to go get their shoes on and get in the car to go to school, and they don't move. (As if they didn't hear us or see us. Hmmm, sounds a little bit like the responses to the Sympathetic Nervous System, doesn't it?) We reprimand them for disobeying us or not following directions and making the whole family late for school. Now WE'VE become a part of that **perceived** threat. Oops. And going through this type of scenario enough times teaches our child's brain that the FREEZE response isn't removing that perceived threat, because we are still making them go to school. Well, the human brain is resourceful and it figures if FREEZE doesn't work, it will escalate to the next best option: FLIGHT

2. FLIGHT: This is where the Tendon Guard Response (TGR) could really start to come in handy. Let's revisit the above scenario where we tell our child to go get their shoes on and get in the car to go to school. But they've learned that FREEZE isn't going to protect them from going to school, so they're going to transition into FLIGHT instead. There are primarily two different ways this could play out. First, your child goes to their bedroom to get their shoes on, and never returns (flees out of your sight in the hopes that you won't actually come find them and make them go to school). OR, your child goes to their bedroom to get their shoes on, walks out the door to get in the car, then runs down the block, literally fleeing you. Why are they running from you, the parent who loves them and protects them and guides them? Remember in the FREEZE phase above when we accidentally became part of the threat? At this point, we still

don't know a better way to respond and we catch our child (either figuratively by finding them in their room, or literally by physically catching them as they're running away). And we reprimand them for disobeying us or not following directions and making the whole family late for school, and this time possibly for endangering themselves and/or others. And now we're *really* connected to the perceived threat of school. And if this happens enough times, your child's brain figures out that the FLIGHT response isn't protecting them from the **perceived** threat either, so the only thing left to do is FIGHT.

3. FIGHT: Sigh. This is the really tough one. This could literally look like physical hitting, kicking, biting, spitting, clawing, scratching, etc. Or it could look like conflict-seeking behavior. For example, you say the sky is blue, they say it's red just to disagree with you. Why in the world would they disagree about something so ridiculous? Because you, Mom or Dad, accidentally, unintentionally, and repeatedly connected yourself to the **perceived** threat. And now you are no longer perceived as a safe harbor, at least in this situation (getting shoes, putting them on and getting in the car to go to school) and possibly not in other situations either. I did it too. And I didn't learn any better until my kids were in their teens.

There IS hope to change these patterns! And I'm going to help you learn how very soon! But first I want you to understand why you may not have gotten this type of help before. Especially if you've had your child in special education, or on medication, or in various therapies.

It's sadly true that many professionals don't understand this process. And they are particularly unaware of the effect of an active Fear Paralysis Reflex and/or an active Moro Reflex (mentioned on page 16). I have worked with the children of other healthcare professionals, including pediatricians, who have told me that until they brought their child to me, they had **never** heard this information before. Not even in med school. Much like you, they just didn't know that they didn't know. Neither did I, until I had a need in my own family. And what they, and I, **did** know was how to scaffold, or support development of skills-acquisition and knowledge-acquisition externally, rather than changing processing internally. I'll show you what I mean.

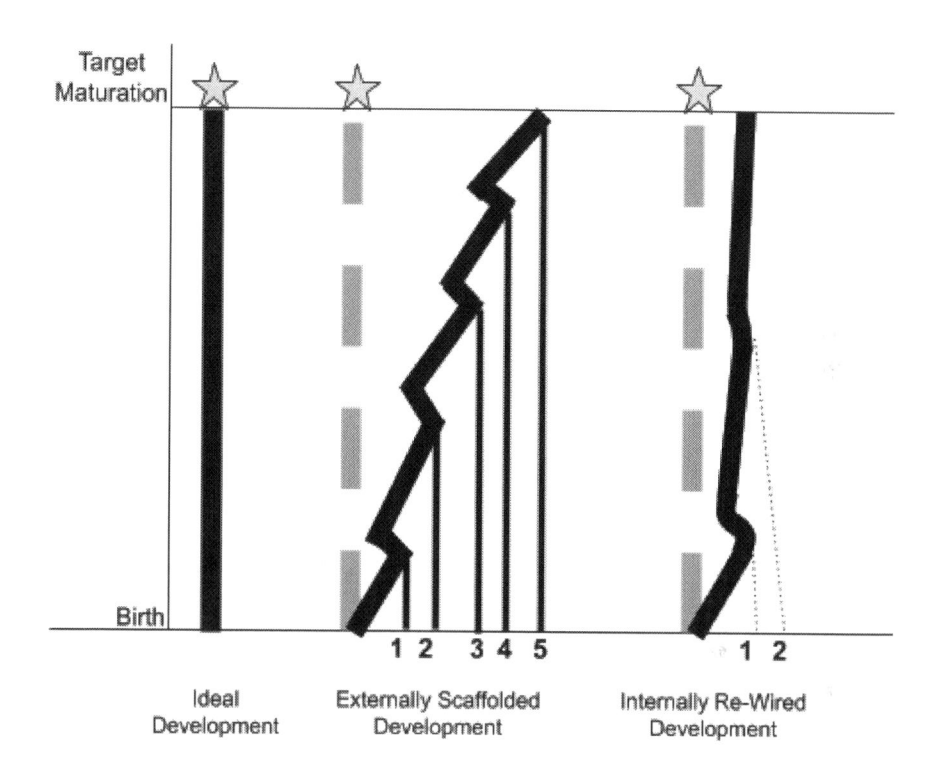

Target Maturation

Ideal Development	Externally Scaffolded Development	Internally Re-Wired Development
	1 2 3 4 5	1 2

The solid line represents "Ideal Development" from birth to full maturity. No one on earth can claim "Ideal Development". We have all taken detours and some detours from "Ideal Development" are large enough that professional intervention is required.

You can see in the "Externally Scaffolded Development" that the child began to detour from the "Ideal Development" pattern (dotted line) and was propped up with an external support (examples: sitting near the teacher's desk in class for behavior monitoring, behavior management chart with rewards, medications, etc.) None of these interventions is wrong. But they also didn't change the child's developmental foundation or how they processed information. Nor does the child "own" any of them - they are <u>put upon</u> him rather than being <u>internally managed by</u> him. And each time he's scaffolded it brings him closer to "Ideal Development". But he didn't actually change how he processed input (ex: learning to use calming techniques to calm himself before lashing out at a classmate when he felt anxious or scared) and he will likely continue to require external regulation for those times he feels anxious or scared. I call these external regulation supports a "top-down" approach to skill acquisition because they are placed upon the child.

In the "Internally Re-Wired Development" scenario, intervention was still required, but less often because the developmental foundation was realigned and processing skills were improved. (Using the above example, a child who has learned calming techniques and can self-regulate by using those techniques no longer has to sit next to the teacher's desk or utilize a behavior chart for external regulation of their behavior.) They are now better able to take the skills they learn earlier and generalize them to more challenging tasks as they grow. Once a solid foundation of stress management skills are in place, (barring any other obstacles such as active immature reflexes), then the individual is better able to achieve development of skills-acquisition and knowledge-acquisition. I call this a "bottom-up" approach to skill acquisition, because it involves restructuring the foundation of how the input is processed. Oh, and that second, minor intervention in the graph? That's when hormones kick in. Everything goes a little nuts then. Don't worry, the earlier gains can be recaptured.

For most children, a combination of "top-down" and "bottom-up" approaches to skill acquisition works best. Allowing a child to have more immediate success at tasks by providing the scaffolding they need, while simultaneously working on developmental processing will eventually produce lifelong skills that can be generalized to other situations and tasks.

A calm brain is better able to communicate, socialize, learn, and engage in healthy relationships. This is the first step in my unique treatment approach in my office. A brain at peace can be molded much more efficiently than a stressed or anxious brain.

Now, let's move on to discuss WHO can benefit and HOW MUCH can be done to decrease the stress response.

4 How to Get the Most Benefit from this Book

ALL of the techniques in this book can be useful tools for anyone, any age, as long as there are no precautionary conditions involved. (I'm going to reiterate the Medical Disclaimer from the front of this book. This book is not intended to be a substitute for professional medical advice, diagnosis, or treatment. Always seek the advice of your physician or other qualified health provider with any questions you may have regarding a medical condition. Never disregard professional medical advice or delay in seeking it because of something you have read in this book.)

We all recognize the saying, "Put your oxygen mask on first before you try to help others." Face it, you can't give what you don't have. If you are stressed, you will have little patience to use these techniques to help your child. And you're not hiding your stress - your kids *can* sense it. But, if you as the parent start to implement these tools and techniques, not only will you be modeling good self care and behavior management, YOU will actually start to feel calmer, better regulated, and better able to support your child's stress response!

As a general rule, these techniques are best used as a maintenance type of tool. In other words, use them *before* you get to the point of no return to hopefully decrease (or dare I say *eliminate*?) the occurrence of the meltdowns. But a few of the techniques can be used during a Fight, Flight, Freeze event. I'll indicate which ones when I discuss **How much? How Often? How long?** to practice each technique.

It is important to keep in mind that none of these techniques, either alone or combined, are a magic wand. Children *will* have emotions and they *will* act them out. And sometimes all we can do is be there for them while they go through those big emotions. There is no way to rush out of a Fight, Flight, Freeze response. That's why it's best to do what we can to calm the brain *before* something triggers that response, so that hopefully, it's a much smaller, shorter duration, and much more manageable response.

It is our job as parents and professionals to teach them a better way. But until our better ways become internal regulation tools for them, we have to be their loving, gentle, external regulation.

The techniques are categorized based on type of technique.

1. Spiritual
2. Hydration
3. Whole Brain Activation
4. Breath Control
5. Sensory Stimuli
    a. Tactile & Proprioception: Touch and deep pressure, awareness of body position in space, and/or muscle contraction
    b. Vestibular: Balance and movement (acceleration, deceleration, slope, rotation)
    c. Auditory: sound
    d. Visual: sight
    e. Olfactory & Gustatory: smell (goes directly to the midbrain where emotions and memory are controlled) and taste.
    f. Interoception: internal awareness of state of being(bowel/bladder, digestion, etc.); mindfulness
6. Behavioral
7. Physiological
8. Alternative

The more approaches we can combine at once to help us or our child calm, the better we will be able to access those calming mechanisms in the future. Neurons that fire together, wire together! (Hebb's axiom, paraphrased.) Here are a few examples of how to combine strategies.

1. Performing yoga outdoors could utilize:
    a. Spiritual if you choose.
    b. Whole Brain Activation for some poses that require crossing midline.
    c. Breath Control
    d. Sensory: Tactile & Proprioception with the poses
    e. Sensory: Vestibular from poses that require head movements in certain planes and/or inversion.
    f. Sensory: Auditory from the outdoor sounds (birds, water, music, etc.)
    g. Sensory: Olfactory from the outdoor scents (grass, trees, flowers, water, etc.)
    h. Sensory: Interoception if you choose mindfulness activities during yoga (such as awareness of breaths).

2. Laying on a therapy ball on their belly while playing with scented dough and listening to music could utilize:
    a. Sensory: Tactile & Proprioception when utilizing their arms to support their body weight as well as to manipulate the dough.
    b. Sensory: Vestibular (inversion) when their head is below their center of gravity.
    c. Sensory: Auditory from the music
    d. Sensory: Olfactory from the scented dough
    e. Sensory: Interoception from pressure on the internal organs while laying over the ball.

3. Kneeling on a grounding mat while blowing a bubble volcano located in front of their knees could utilize:
    a. Breath Control
    b. Sensory: Tactile & Proprioception: from holding themselves using trunk muscles, or using their hands to prop themselves above the bubble volcano
    c. Sensory: Auditory from the sound of the bubbles being blown in the soap solution.

d. Sensory: Visual from the sight of the bubbles overflowing the container.
e. Sensory: Olfactory from the smell of the soap solution
f. Physiological from the possible shift in electrical charge from the grounding mat.

5 Fight, Flight, Freeze Reduction Techniques

PRAYER AND MEDITATION

Several research studies have linked religion and spirituality with decreased stress. Whether you believe in God or not, you can be spiritual. Spirituality can be defined as "the quality of being concerned with the human spirit or soul as opposed to material or physical things."

Prayer and meditation can help us calm our minds by focusing on one thing. Repetition of familiar prayer can keep our minds from wandering, and offer some comfort from the familiar.

We will also likely calm our breathing (Breath Control) and receive proprioceptive input (See Sensory, page 33) while praying or meditating. And if we listen to music or calming noises (ex: falling rain), or repeat sounds (reciting prayer out loud or repeating "OM") we can stimulate our Auditory system. We will stimulate our Vestibular system via vibration from our larynx. If we visually focus on one item (ex: cross, flame on a candle), and use incense or essential oils, we can stimulate our Visual, and Olfactory sensory systems in a calming manner as well. The multi-sensory input will help us recall a sense of calm more quickly in the future when we are presented with that same sensory input again.

How much? How often? How long? Prayer and/or meditation can literally be done anytime, anywhere. It can be utilized but should not be forced during a Fight, Flight, Freeze event.

HYDRATION

Our brains and bodies are electric, and utilize water to conduct the impulses. Dehydration impedes those impulses. According to the United States Geological Survey, "up to 60% of the adult human body is made up of water", but the brain alone is composed of 73% water."

Benefits of being well-hydrated for Autonomic Nervous System function:
- Helps to regulate our internal body temperature via sweat and respiration.
- Helps transport nutrients and waste in the bloodstream.
- Flushes waste.
- Required for the brain to manufacture hormones and neurotransmitters.
- Helps conduct electrical activity between neurons.

The amount of daily water intake each one of us needs varies depending upon our size, the weather, and our activities. And just plain old water is best. Drinks with added sugars will make it harder for your child to regulate their metabolism and mood.

Here are some suggestions to get your child to drink more liquids:
- Serve it in small doses. Dixie cups work well.

- Provide a straw. Keep in mind that straws can be cut into any size, so if your child struggles to suck water through the full length of a straw, just cut it!
- Add their favorite fruits to the water.
- Add their favorite fruit-flavored snack or candy. My kids used to add Skittles to their water. I didn't love that, but they drank it.
- Provide a water cooler with a dispenser spigot. There are some very inexpensive, refillable ones that will fit in your refrigerator.
- Offer an alternative to water. Smoothies sweetened with honey can be appealing to a child with a sweet tooth. Caffeine-free teas with fruit and/or honey are good options as well. There are also dairy products (milks, kefirs, etc.), and low- or no-sugar sports drinks to consider.

How much? How often? How long? As stated above, the answers to these questions depend on a variety of factors. It can be utilized during a Fight, Flight, Freeze event with caution for it being a choking hazard for a child not able to calm enough to swallow safely.

WHOLE BRAIN ACTIVATION

There is a great deal of information available to support the benefits of activating the whole brain. Benefits such as increasing calm and focus, improved academic skills for higher test scores, and better coordination for improved sports performance! And there are many professionals and businesses who will tell you that they have the key to helping you make both sides of your child's brain work better together. And they probably can. But, keep in mind, Mom and Dad, that *you* can do so much of it on your own, at home, for **FREE**! Or at least inexpensively!

If you do feel the need to seek professional assistance or guidance, I strongly encourage you to find an experienced Occupational Therapist. Or at the very least, make sure the person working directly with your child is a licensed professional, or certified teacher, who fully understands child development, the parts of the brain, and how to promote neural growth.

So why do we want to promote whole brain activation? In a nutshell, to give your child more resources to draw from when they are stressed. It's the difference between a full plate of a healthy variety of foods to nourish a body, and half a plate with only the potatoes and some veggies available to provide nourishment. It's still good stuff, but it's not optimal.

The best way to promote neural growth to get both sides of the brain communicating better together is to move both sides of the body in a repetitive, rhythmic, coordinated fashion while crossing midline. Remember, that's the *best* way. But maybe your child struggles to cross midline. That's OK. We can back it down a notch or two, or more if needed. Keep it simple and build up to more challenging moves.

1. **Crawl**: One thing we love to do in our office is hide animals around the office and have the kids go on a "Safari", but they have to crawl slooooowly so they don't scare the animals. This requires them to

have to concentrate on their limb movements and hopefully be more intentional about what they move and when they move it.

How much? How often? How long? Anytime for as long as your child enjoys the activity and isn't fatigued. I suggest giving frequent rest breaks as it can be stressful on wrists that aren't used to holding weight. It's best used as a maintenance technique and not during a Fight, Flight, Freeze event.

2. **Knee swings**: have your child lay down on their back, bend their with their feet flat on the bed/floor, and slowly and rhythmically swing their knees side-to-side together. Doing this to slow music will help with the rhythm, and provide auditory stimulation at the same time.

    How much? How often? How long? Bedtime might be a good time to do this activity, especially if you include slow music. This should be an enjoyable or pleasant experience for your child. If it's not, don't do it. If it causes any pain, don't do it. I'd suggest starting with 5 to each side, and work up to a maximum of 10 repetitions. It's best used as a maintenance technique and not during a Fight, Flight, Freeze event.

3. **Pat-A-Cake** or other clapping games
    How much? How often? How long? Anytime for as long as your child enjoys the activity and isn't fatigued. It should feel like play and not work. It's best used as a maintenance technique and not during a Fight, Flight, Freeze event.

4. **Cross Crawls**: Have your child touch their hand or elbow to their opposite knee by bringing their knee up to meet their hand/elbow. This can be done while sitting if

Standing Cross Crawls

balance is a challenge. Or it can be done while standing.
How much? How often? How long? Can be done anytime, but a good time to do this is before school to prep them for the day ahead. Start with 5 repetitions and work up; 25 repetitions is the most I would recommend at one time. Once or twice a day, 3-5 days a week is sufficient. It's best used as a maintenance technique and not during a Fight, Flight, Freeze event.

5. **<u>Rainbow infinity symbol on a vertical surface</u>**: This is sometimes called a "Lazy 8". Tape a piece of paper to the wall or door, and have your child draw an infinity symbol on it. Then have them trace the symbol repeatedly with different colored markers or crayons. You could also do this on a shower wall with soap crayons while your child is taking an epsom salt bath. The trick is to get the infinity symbol positioned in front of them so that they are right in front of the point that it crosses.

    How much? How often? How long? Can be done anytime, but a good time to do this is before school to prep them for the day ahead. Start with 5 repetitions and work up; 10 repetitions is the most I would recommend at one time. One to three times a week is sufficient, but can be done more if they enjoy it. It's best used as a maintenance technique and not during a Fight, Flight, Freeze event.

6. **Sports** that require coordinated, rhythmic, reciprocal movements. Examples would be walking, running, dancing, biking, and martial arts.

   How much? How often? How long? This would depend on how much your child enjoys it, and/or the class or practice schedule. For instance, your child may just enjoy dancing at the house, or riding their bike down the street. It's best used as a maintenance technique and not during a Fight, Flight, Freeze event.

BREATH CONTROL

When we are stressed or anxious, we tend to limit our breathing to shallow, more rapid breaths that are controlled by our shoulders rather than our diaphragm. If we can control our breathing to get deeper, slower breaths by using our diaphragm, we expand our ribcage and diaphragm and stimulate proprioceptors which increase feelings of calm. In addition, the oxygen to carbon dioxide ratio is optimized, and heart rate and blood pressure decrease.

Diaphragmatic breathing and/or an 8-second exhale are where the benefits of breath control kick in. In yoga, breath control is referred to as pranayama, and there are several ways to practice it. The key is to achieve a diaphragmatic inhalation, expanding the belly, and a longer exhalation, typically 8-seconds or longer. This longer exhalation serves to trigger the Vagus nerve to stimulate the Parasympathetic Nervous System which is the "Rest and Digest" side of the Autonomic Nervous System (vs the Sympathetic Nervous System which is the Fight, Flight, Freeze side of the Autonomic Nervous System).

However, most young children would struggle to attempt the breath control techniques utilized in yoga. Fortunately, there are some fun ways to encourage children to take deep belly expanding breaths and to blow out with extended exhalations. Here are a few that have worked with many of my clients:

1. **<u>Blow bubbles:</u>** having a small bottle of bubbles in your purse or the child's backpack is an easy way to engage in blowing bubbles anywhere! Think about places you have to wait with your child: in line at the grocery store, getting a haircut, etc. Allowing your child to blow bubbles will make the wait much more tolerable by calming your child with deep breaths *and* the magic of bubbles!
How much? How often? How long? Anytime for as long as your child enjoys the activity and isn't fatigued or out of breath. It should feel like play and not work. Daily would be a reasonable goal. It's

best used as a maintenance technique and not during a Fight, Flight, Freeze event.

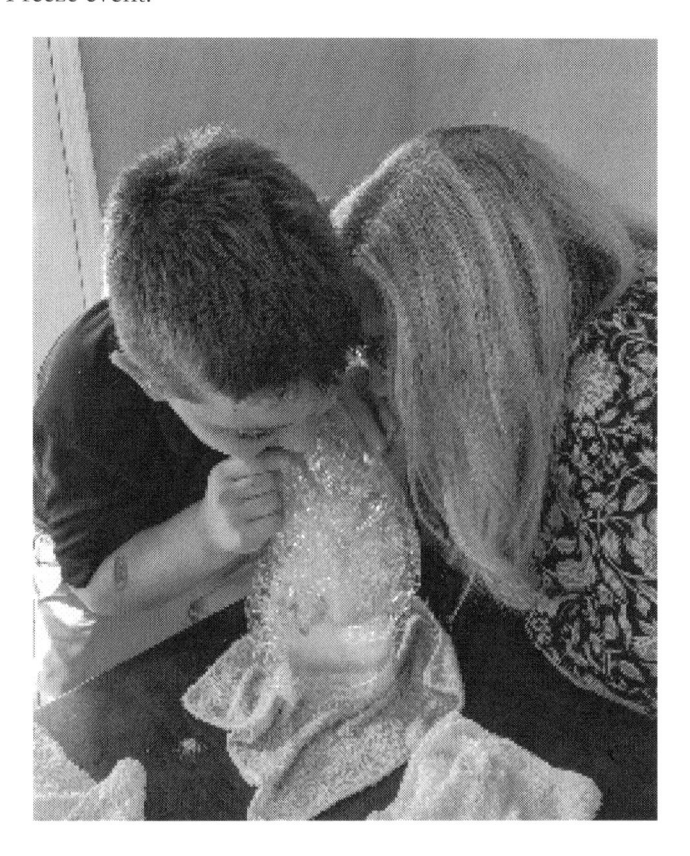

2. **Bubble Volcano:** Fill a somewhat tall container approximately ¾ or more full of water. Put some dishwashing soap in it - a half a teaspoon should be enough. (You can always add more if you need to.). Put a bendy straw in the container and have your child blow and blow and blow! The bubbles will overflow the container and flow down like lava!
Be sure they don't accidentally suck in the bubble water!
    o   For an added bonus, have them scoop up handfuls of the bubbles and clap their hands! They will be stimulating their

Proprioceptive and Vestibular sensory systems, and the bubbles will "explode" and float down like snow!
- ○ The smell from the dish soap might be a pleasant olfactory stimulus.
- ○ Doing this with your child brings you both closer, with a shared goal, and likely shared smiles, creating a stronger connection between you and your child. Aww.

How much? How often? How long? Anytime for as long as your child enjoys the activity and isn't fatigued or out of breath. Four or five times a week would be a reasonable goal. It should feel like play and not work. It's best used as a maintenance technique and not during a Fight, Flight, Freeze event.

3. **Blow Q-tips through straws:** This is akin to blowing darts. Have a large bucket, tub, or bowl ready to be the target. Stick one side of a Q-tip into the end of the straw, and have your child blow through the other end until the Q-tip launches!
Two notes:
   1. Cheaper/generic Q-tips work better because there tends to be less cotton on the ends and they are easier to blow out.
   2. This technique does not do a great job facilitating a long exhale, but it does encourage a deep, belly-expanding breath.bc

How much? How often? How long? Anytime for as long as your child enjoys the activity and isn't fatigued or out of breath. Four or five times a week would be a reasonable goal. It should feel like play and not work. It's best used as a maintenance technique and not during a Fight, Flight, Freeze event.

4. **Propel Cotton balls/Pompoms:** Blow through a straw to propel cotton balls or pompoms. Here a few activities to make this engaging for your child:

a. Have a puff ball race. Your child and another person (you?) should be on your knees at the starting line. Holding the straw in your mouths with your lips/teeth, crawl along the "race track" blowing a cotton ball/pompom to the finish line.
   b. Have a battle: Throw the cotton balls/pompoms on the floor, or on a tabletop. Sit across from each other. Blow through a straw to propel the cotton balls/pompoms across an imaginary goal line or off of the table. See who blew more cotton balls/pompoms onto the other's side.
   c. Make a safari trail with painter's tape on the floor. Have your child blow the cotton ball/pompom along the trail to find the "animals".

   How much? How often? How long? Anytime for as long as your child enjoys the activity and isn't fatigued or out of breath. Four or five times a week would be a reasonable goal. It should feel like play and not work. It's best used as a maintenance technique and not during a Fight, Flight, Freeze event.

5. **<u>Singing</u>** often requires deep breaths and long exhalations with the lyrics. Suggested songs:
   a. Alphabet song
   b. Twinkle, Twinkle Little Star
   c. Row, Row, Row Your Boat
   d. Itsy Bitsy Spider
   e. This Little Light of Mine
   f. Jesus Loves Me

   How much? How often? How long? Anytime for as long as your child enjoys the activity and isn't fatigued or out of breath. Daily would be a reasonable goal. It should be enjoyable and not feel like work. It's best used as a maintenance technique and not during a Fight, Flight, Freeze event.

6. **<u>Weather Breathing</u>** utilizes imagery that the child is likely familiar with to describe the 3 types of breath that they will attempt to control. They can do this lying down on their backs, or sitting up.

Instruct the child to imagine a big hurricane swirling inside of them. They are going to attempt to blow that hurricane out to sea with the following breaths:
    - Hurricane Breath: Tell them to take a BIG deep breath in through their open ***mouth*** that makes their bellies get bigger! Then have them blow out through ***pursed lips*** (as if blowing out a candle flame) until they feel like there's almost no air left inside their lungs! After 2-3 of these Hurricane Breaths, tell them that the hurricane is starting to move away, but there are still some thunderstorms inside of them that need to be blown away.
    - Stormy Day Breaths: Tell them to close their mouth, and take a deep breath in through their ***nose***, still making their bellies get bigger. Then blow out through ***pursed lips*** to blow those storms away. Do this type of breathing 2-3 times.
    - Sunny Day Breaths: Now tell your child that they have successfully blown the storms away, and there is now a sunny day breeze blowing inside of them. This is a calm, pleasant breeze that makes the leaves on the trees rustle and move a little, and makes the grass gently sway. At this point, the breaths should be deep, but not as deep as the Hurricane or Stormy Day breaths. They should be calm, even breaths in through their ***nose***, and out through their ***nose***. Encourage them to enjoy the visualization of the Sunny Day imagery while their nervous system turns the volume down on any

Sympathetic Nervous System activity and turns it up on the Parasympathetic Nervous System.

How much? How often? How long? This technique is best used in practice on a daily basis if your child can follow the instructions and utilize the imagery. It can be most beneficial during a build-up to a Fight, Flight, Freeze event as a preventative, but may be helpful during a Fight, Flight, Freeze event as well.

SENSORY

I am not going to go too deep into a description of Sensory Processing or the sensory systems, but a brief explanation is necessary for you to more easily adopt the techniques below. I will briefly describe the sensory system, then give you suggestions for stimulating the calming effect from that sensory system.

We are all probably familiar with the 5 basic senses that we are taught in elementary school, but not many of us know that we actually have 8 senses:

The Tactile and Proprioceptive Senses

Proprioception is God's sensory gift to us. It's the sensory system that helps us calm down and focus. The receptors are located in our muscle bellies and tendons, and in our joints. They serve to let us know where our body parts are, and what they are doing, ie, are they moving; are they holding something heavy like a gallon of milk or something light like an egg? And these receptors get triggered when we stretch our muscles (as in reaching our hands up over our heads), when we contract our muscles (as in when we carry something heavy, or we squeeze someone we love in a big bear hug), and when we squeeze or compress our bodies (as in when we receive a big bear hug, or when we wear tight clothing).

Tactile processing refers to the sense of touch. This sensory system can be alerting (like when a bug lands on your arm) or discriminating (being able to sense the difference between scratchy wool fabric and smooth silk fabric).

These two sensory systems work very well with each other because they often react to the same stimulus. For example, when you hug someone, you feel their touch on your skin and your tactile receptors are stimulated, and you sense their pressure against your muscles thereby stimulating the proprioceptors.

How much? How often? How long? I will give separate suggestions for each technique below, but in general, Proprioceptive input is believed to have a 2 hour effect, that gradually fades to nothing. And since it is typically experienced as pleasurable to most people, there is very little risk of doing it too much. (However, if your child does not like it, don't do it! That would be counterproductive to calming.) Since the Tactile system tends to be more alerting, it's best not to over-stimulate it. So, if you are doing a combined Proprioceptive and Tactile technique, approximately every 2 hours or longer would probably be sufficient as a maintenance for avoiding an adverse response. I don't recommend stimulating only the Tactile system. It's too "touchy". (Get it? Haha!)

Below are some activities that will stimulate our proprioceptive systems, and often our tactile systems as well:

1. **Yoga.** Many yoga poses require us to contract our muscles, and to hold that muscle contraction for an extended period of time, thus firing the proprioceptors repeatedly as we continue to maintain muscle contraction. In addition, the tactile system can sense the clothing we wear and the feel of the surface we are practicing yoga on.

    I like to use Frog Yoga Alphabet in my office with the kids. You can find FREE downloadables here:

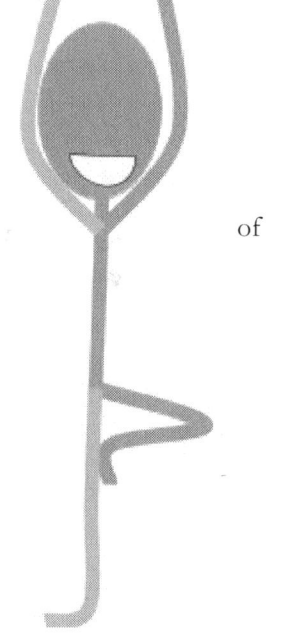

    https://youngyogamasters.com/2014/05/28/yoga-alphabet-printable/ or you can search for "Frog alphabet yoga free download".

How much? How often? How long? Yoga can be done virtually anytime, anywhere within energy levels. Be careful not to over-fatigue your child. Yoga is best used as a maintenance technique and not during a Fight, Flight, Freeze response.

2. **Hugs**. We call this "Vitamin H" in my house, and everyone gets a liberal dose FIRST thing in the morning! This way, no one has gotten mad at anyone yet, nor is anyone awake enough to resist the hug (think teenagers). And you get the added bonus of skin contact (tactile stimulus), the look of your barely awake child with slightly disheveled hair and squinty eyes (visual input), the sound of your child's breath/moans/groans from having to be awake (auditory

input) and the smell of your child (good or bad, it's olfactory input) so you and your child are experiencing a multi-sensory activity through the simple act of hugging!

- I understand that this may seem like an unpleasant task for some. Maybe you KNOW your child is unpleasant in the morning and the thought of approaching them with arms wide open seems futile, and possibly painful. And maybe it is, for now. It was NOT natural for me or my family either. But after many, many, many, many attempts and poor excuses for hugs (their arms hung limp at their sides, not reciprocating my hug at all) we finally got to a point where they came to not just expect it and tolerate it, but they now reciprocate with their arms wrapped around me in a big, tight squeeze! They are in their early 20's now. I'd say the reciprocated hugs started showing up in their late teens. It took a looooonnngggg time. Don't give up!

How much? How often? How long? We do it daily, and then some. I don't believe you can over-hug anyone, as long as they aren't averse to it. This can be used as a maintenance technique, or to calm a Fight, Flight, Freeze response. However, be aware of your child's squeeze-tolerance! You don't want to make them feel like they are being suffocated by a Boa Constrictor!

3. **Knee Squishes**: Proprioception is provided via the receptors in our lower back, hips, knees, ankles, and feet with this technique. Tactile stimulation is provided via your hands on their knees, and the feel of the surface they are lying on. I have found this technique to be very helpful for many children.

Have your child lie down on the floor, a mat, or bed with bent knees and feet flat. Imagine a plumb line going down from your child's knees. Now, place your hands GENTLY on top of their knees and push straight down, in line with that imaginary plumb line. DO NOT push toward the hips and DO NOT push toward the feet. This should cause NO PAIN or DISCOMFORT to your child.

How much? How often? How long? Approximately 15-20 squishes, twice a day should be sufficient for a maintenance program. It can be used during a Fight, Flight, Freeze event, with extreme caution so as not to injure the child. If in doubt, don't use it.

4. **Child Sandwich**: For this technique, you will need 2 pillows. Tell the child you're making a "Child's name" sandwich and that they get to choose what goes on it. Let them know that they will get to be in control of making the sandwich, to include when it's finished. Lay one pillow on a firm surface like the floor. Have your child lay on that pillow on their belly (facing down). Then ask them what they want on their sandwich. Whatever they choose to put on their sandwich, you figuratively apply to the back of their body. For instance, if they want peanut butter, pretend that your hand is the knife spreading peanut butter all over the back of their body. If they want banana, press firmly with your open palm on the back of their body figuratively placing banana slices on the sandwich, if they want sliced cheese, lay your hand and forearm firmly across different areas of the back of their body. Be creative. When they are finished

adding the insides of the sandwich, put the 2nd pillow on top of them. Let them choose if they want to be finished at this point, or if they want a "pressed sandwich". If they choose to be a "pressed sandwich", apply firm pressure to the top pillow, being sure that they can still breathe comfortably. Allow them to decide when they're done. This technique sometimes requires a demonstration before the child is comfortable being the sandwich.

How much? How often? How long? Can be done as much as desired. This technique is beneficial as a maintenance technique, and could be helpful during a Fight, Flight, Freeze event.

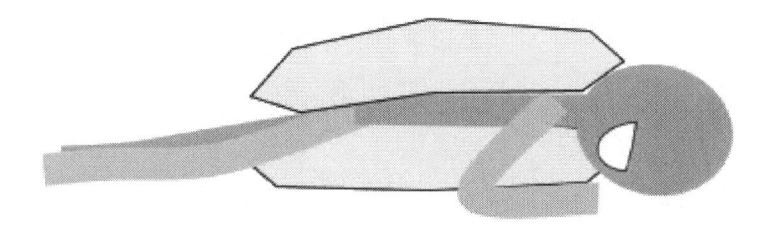

5. **Balance on one foot**: Add a Breath Control technique to provide additional calming input. Have them count out loud if they want to. Or have them sing, thereby stimulating the auditory system and vestibular system via singing **and** via balancing on one foot at the same time!

    How much? How often? How long? I'd suggest having your child try to balance on one foot for 10 seconds initially, then gradually increase it by 5-10 seconds until they can do 1 minute. This can be used as a maintenance technique, but likely won't be effective during a Fight, Flight, Freeze event.

6. **Head Rakes**: Consist of 5 different tracing patterns starting on the face and ending at the crown of the head. Place thumbs where indicated by shaded circles, and remaining fingers should rest on the hairline around the face. All fingers/thumbs move from the starting point up to the crown of the head using light, but firm pressure. A circular massage at the temples, cheeks (masseter muscle) and/or ears can be additionally relaxing. These areas are indicated by the stars. (If you would like to do this to yourself, or your child would like to do this by themselves, the only difference is with the first pattern that

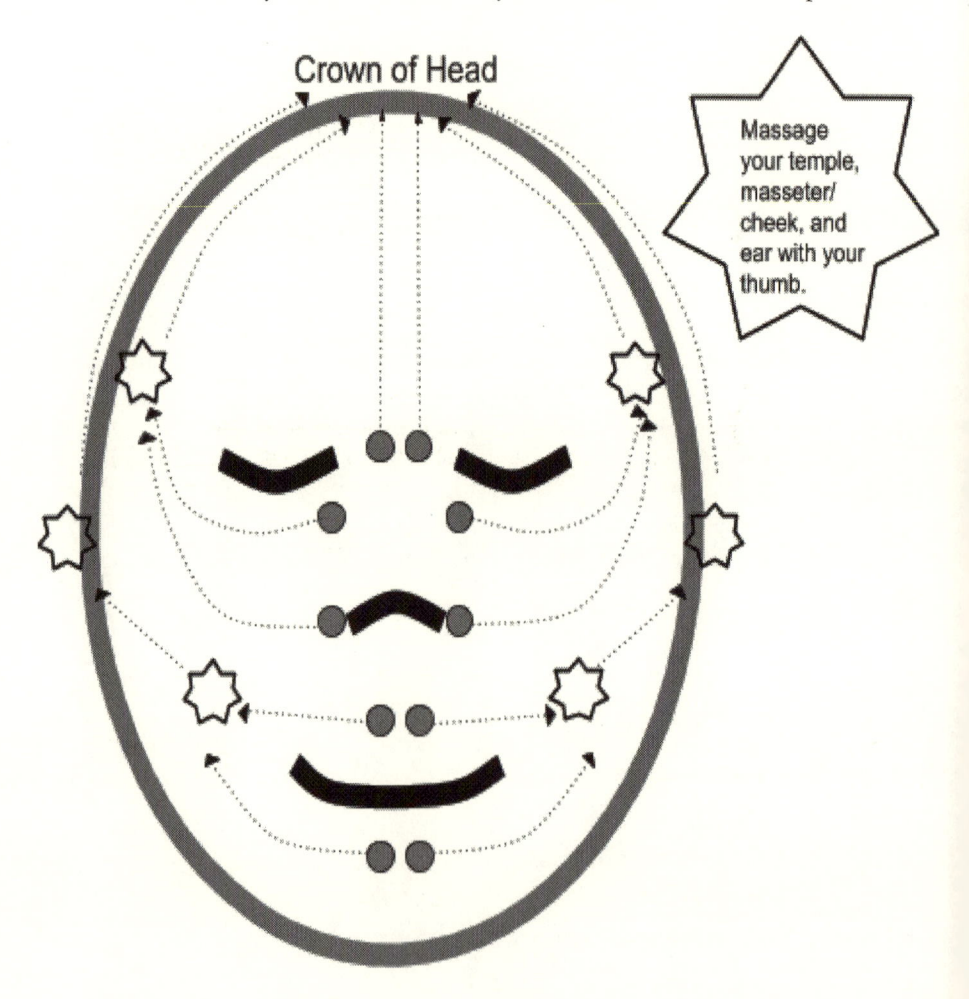

Crown of Head

Massage your temple, masseter/cheek, and ear with your thumb.

starts between the eyes. You would put your own pinkies on the shaded circles, then follow the dotted lines to the crown of the head. The other patterns start with the thumb on the shaded circles.

How much? How often? How long? 3-5 repetitions, 2-3 times a day maximum. Only if they are not averse to it. It might be helpful during a Fight, Flight, Freeze event.

7. **Bin of beans**: Fill a bin with beans and let your child play in it. Ideally you want it to have beans deep enough to immerse their hands above their wrists. We have filled a large bin with 20 lbs of beans, and let kids sit in them.

    How much? How often? How long? Can be done as much as desired. This technique is beneficial as a maintenance technique, and could be helpful during a Fight, Flight, Freeze event.

8. **Massages**: Massages are universally understood to be relaxing. However, for someone with sensory processing dysfunction, they may actually be alerting to the point that they would create a Fight, Flight, Freeze response. Be sure you have permission to touch your child before you attempt to massage them. And it may be helpful to start with "safe" areas such as the hands. Stop immediately if they indicate that it makes them uncomfortable.

    How much? How often? How long? 2-3 times a day should be sufficient for maintenance. You might be able to calm your child while they are in the middle of a Fight, Flight, Freeze event by providing a massage to their hands or feet.

9. **Burrito**: Have your child roll himself up in a blanket or yoga mat. Be very careful that they do not roll themselves too tightly. I'd suggest keeping their arms out of the "burrito". This should be a pleasurable experience for your child. If it isn't, don't do it!
   How much? How often? How long? 30 seconds to 2 minutes twice a day, up to 5 days a week. This can be used as a maintenance technique, but do not use it during a Fight, Flight, Freeze event.

   Blanket wrapped loosely around child, jelly-roll style.

10. **Prayer Push**: Have your child hold their hands together palm-to-palm as if in a prayer pose, then have them alternate pushing their palms together and relaxing.

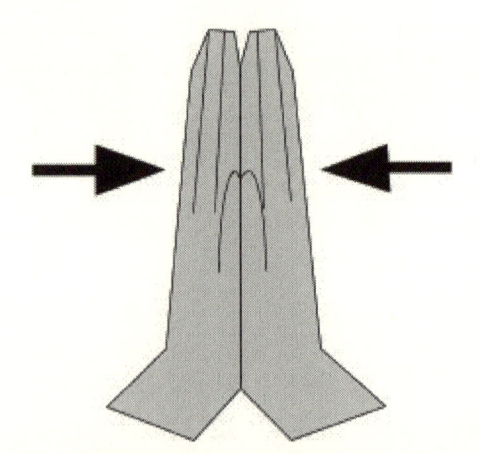

    How much? How often? How long? Can be done anytime, anywhere. Can be done as a maintenance technique, but would likely be beneficial during a Fight, Flight, Freeze event.

11. **Oral sensory input**: The proprioceptors in the muscles in our cheeks, and the tactile receptors and proprioceptors inside and around our mouths are stimulated when we chew or crunch on something. Generally, chewy items (gum, dried fruits, Chewelry, potable water tubing, etc.) tend to have a more focusing effect than crunching or sucking. Crunching on popcorn, ice chips, hard candy, etc. is actually considered to be alerting, and can be utilized to help someone who may be falling asleep or is bored. And sucking on something (thumbs, pacifiers, thick liquids like milkshakes/smoothies/ applesauce, or lollipops, etc.) is generally calming.

> **Sucking = Calming**
>
> **Chewing = Focusing**
>
> **Crunching = Alerting**

How much? How often? How long? This could be done throughout the day, but is probably best if limited to certain timeframes simply for oral hygiene purposes. I'd say maybe 30 minutes to 1 hour at a time, 3 times a day, aside from meals. However, you may decide that more, or less, is what's appropriate in your family. This can be used as a maintenance technique, and during a Fight, Flight, Freeze event, especially sucking on something to calm.

12. **Carrying heavy items**: Many people claim that lifting weights and working out in general helps them feel grounded and happy.
    a. You can ask your child to help you bring the groceries in from the car and let them carry the milk or laundry detergent.

b. You can fill a laundry basket with heavy items, including siblings!, and have them push it across the floor pretending they are a truck driver, bus driver, or train engineer!
c. You can have them dig a hole in the dirt with a shovel. Plant flowers, shrubs, vegetables, and herbs! Dirt is HEAVY!
d. Fill a pillowcase or old sock with about 2-3 lbs of dry beans or rice. Play catch with the weighted item.
e. Get a 3-5 lb ball and play catch. Have the child add patterns between tosses such as throw the ball up in the air, clap 3 times, then throw the ball.
f. And, lifting weights and exercise would provide proprioceptive input.

How much? How often? How long? Recalling that proprioceptive input has a 2-hour effect, I'd say you could space these activities out every 2 hours or longer. You have to be very aware of your child's fatigue level and respect that. Do not over-fatigue your child with sensory input! This can be used as a maintenance technique, but likely won't be effective during a Fight, Flight, Freeze event.

13. **Being in water**: When we immerse ourselves in water, it exerts pressure on our bodies and we *feel* the water. That pressure stimulates the proprioceptors and increases our sense of calm. We must also consider that most swimwear has an element of compression (elastic waistbands, Rash Guard shirts, etc.) that also provide proprioceptive input. There are many other anecdotal reports of salt water benefitting us in different ways, but the research is scarce.
    How much? How often? How long? This can be done as often as it is tolerated and does not impede health or wellness. This can be used as a maintenance technique, but not during a Fight, Flight, Freeze event.

14. **Play with clay, dough, or putty**: Contracting the muscles of their hands, forearms, and arms will provide proprioceptive input, while allowing them to be creative (a mindfulness activity). The feel of the dough will provide tactile input as well. You could consider adding an Essential Oil to the mixture and stimulate the Olfactory system too!

    How much? How often? How long? Unlimited. This can be used as a maintenance technique, and during a Fight, Flight, Freeze event to help them utilize the creative part of their brain, thereby taking some of the energy from the survival instinct of their brain, and dampening that response.

15. **Digging in the dirt**: Digging in the dirt warrants being mentioned all by itself even though it was mentioned along with "Carrying Heavy Items. It provides a variety of benefits to our brains and bodies. And if you are working/playing in the dirt to produce food, there is an added reward to the sensory input. Digging in the dirt not only provides proprioceptive and tactile input, it also provides visual stimuli, and olfactory/smell stimuli. In addition, there is a bacteria that naturally occurs in dirt that we absorb into our bodies when we play in the dirt. Our bodies metabolize that bacteria and it results in an anti-depressant effect on our brains/mood. This effect has been shown to be as effective as some prescription medications, and is believed to last as long as 3 weeks! (This is NOT intended to be medical advice. Please consult your physician before going off of ANY medication!)

    How much? How often? How long? This is such a wonderful activity that I believe you could let your child do this every day, for hours while their imagination runs away with them. My own children spent 3 weeks digging holes in our back yard deep enough and large enough for them to lay down in them! (Yes, those are my children in the holes they dug in the below pictures!) Again, be aware of your child's fatigue level, and to their hydration needs, possible injury risk, allergies, etc. This can be used as a maintenance technique, but likely won't be effective during a Fight, Flight, Freeze event.

Yes, these are my children. And these are the holes they spent 3 weeks happily digging and playing in!

16. **<u>Power Posing</u>:** There is enough evidence to suggest that certain body positions can make us feel more powerful and thereby, reduce feelings of inadequacy. These positions are largely expansive positions (think Wonder Woman: feet apart, hands on hips, straight upright posture). Rather than me trying to describe the variety of poses, feel free to google this term.
    How much? How often? How long? Unlimited. This can be used as a maintenance technique, and during a Fight, Flight, Freeze event.

The Vestibular System

The most important thing to know about Vestibular Stimuli is that it should **NEVER** be imposed on an individual with a known seizure disorder without professional guidance from a qualified Occupational Therapist.

Vestibular processing refers to the sense of movement and balance. The receptors are located in our inner ears, and they sense acceleration, deceleration, slope, pitch, and rotation. Anyone who has tried to comfort a fussy or crying baby by rocking them or bouncing them instinctively knows that vestibular input can be calming. I actually like to describe it more along the lines of integrating, which has an element of calming to it but recognizes that it helps the brain organize information for functional use. Before we get started, I'm going to reiterate that Vestibular stimuli should **NEVER** be imposed on an individual with a known seizure disorder without professional guidance from a qualified Occupational Therapist.

> **How much? How often? How long?** Vestibular stimuli can be both calming and alerting. Often, the response is dependent on what type of vestibular input is being received and on the individual's processing of that input. A recommendation for Vestibular stimuli is absolutely best provided by a qualified Occupational Therapist who has evaluated your child. But if your child already swings, twirls, jumps, etc, then you probably do not need to impose this type of stimuli upon them. They are getting it on their own. See if you can slow them down and give them better rhythm for the calming effect. If your child avoids Vestibular stimuli, and you do not have access to a qualified Occupational Therapist, I'd recommend starting **very** cautiously and slowly, and watching for adverse reactions. For example, 15-20 seconds of unfamiliar imposed vestibular stimuli, with a 48-hour watch period. Note any unusual behaviors, moods, sleep, digestion, etc. If you see anything unusual, don't impose any more Vestibular stimuli until you have your child evaluated by a qualified

Occupational Therapist. If you do not notice any adverse reactions, increase duration by 5-10 seconds every 48 hours, up to 2 minutes.

Linear vestibular input refers to progressive or repetitive movement in a head-to-toe, front-to-back, or side-to-side direction. For example, riding in a wagon being pulled down the street is a progressive, front-directional, linear vestibular movement. The vestibular receptors are sensing a continuous movement in one direction (along with corresponding information coming in from other senses such as the eyes and ears). A repetitive, back-and-forth movement seems to have a greater calming effect as evidenced by the natural use of this pattern for most of us. Below are some ways to achieve the repetitive type of linear vestibular input:

1. **Rocking** in a rocking chair, glider, or baby swing.
   How much? How often? How long? This should be an enjoyable experience, so if your child doesn't like it, don't do it! For the child who enjoys rocking and already does it frequently, there's little reason to regulate it for them now. Remember, this is not therapy, this is a comforting activity that can help your child calm and regulate. Be sure they aren't going to fall off anything and hurt themselves. This can be used as a maintenance technique and would also be effective during a Fight, Flight, Freeze event.

2. **Swinging** on a swing. Seated would be front-to-back. Laying on the belly or back could be a head-to-toe movement or could be a side-to-side movement, depending on the position of the person and the direction of the swing.
   How much? How often? How long? This should be an enjoyable experience, so if your child doesn't like it, don't do it! Swinging can be alerting for some children, so caution must be exercised with the child who responds this way. I'd suggest starting with 30 seconds, and slowly building up to 5 minutes, 3-5 times a week. For the child who enjoys swinging and already does it frequently, there's little reason to regulate it for them now. Remember, this is not therapy,

this is a fun activity that can help your child calm and regulate. It could be alerting and interrupt sleep if done too close to bedtime. Be careful not to fatigue your child. Be sure they aren't going to fall off anything and hurt themselves. This is best used as a maintenance technique and would also be effective during a Fight, Flight, Freeze event.

3. **Jumping/Bouncing** on a trampoline, seated bouncing on a ball, or jumping on a bed would be an example of head-to-toe repetitive linear vestibular input. This technique would also provide proprioceptive input.
How much? How often? How long? As much as they want if they already enjoy this type of input. For a child who struggles with maintaining an internal rhythm, this is a great start to developing one and thereby reducing the stress response. In that case, start with 10 repetitions to try to attain a good rhythm and symmetry. Build up to 25 in small increments, maintaining rhythm and symmetry. Can be done daily, anytime during the day. It could be alerting and interrupt sleep if done too close to bedtime. Be careful not to fatigue your child. Be sure they aren't going to fall off anything and hurt themselves. This is best used as a maintenance technique and would also be effective during a Fight, Flight, Freeze event.

4. **Rolling** head-to-toe on their belly over a therapy ball.
How much? How often? How long? Start with 5 repetitions and slowly build up to a maximum of 20 repetitions at one time, 3-5 days a week.. However, for the child that enjoys this and does it on their own, there is little reason to limit what they enjoy. Be sure they aren't going to fall off and hurt themselves. It can be done anytime during the day. This is best used as a maintenance technique and would also be effective during a Fight, Flight, Freeze event.

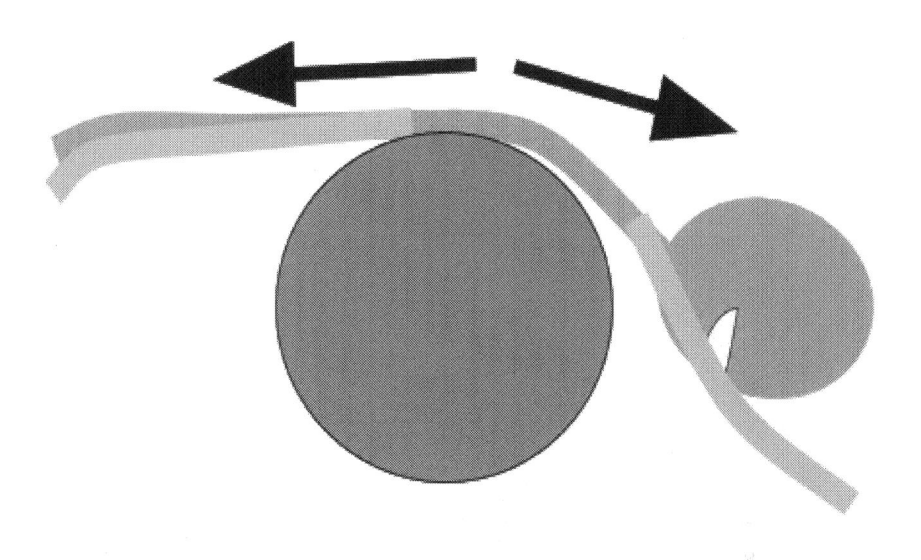

5. **Swaying** head-to-toe or side-to-side while on their hands and knees. This will also provide proprioceptive input with the weight shifting happening in the joints of the arms and legs.

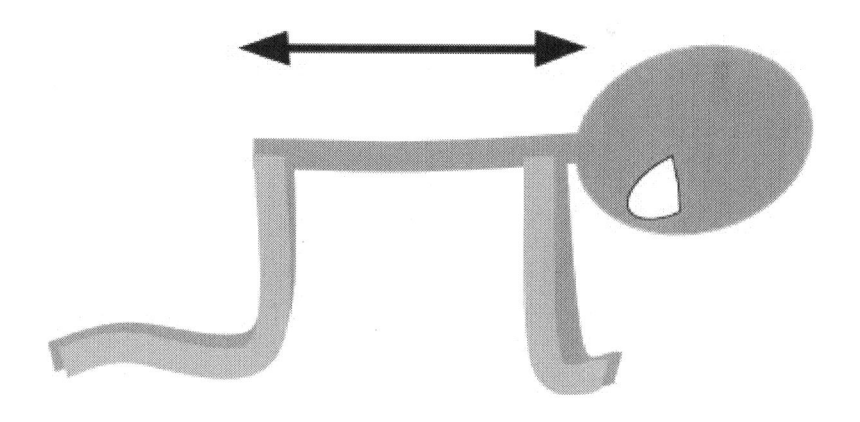

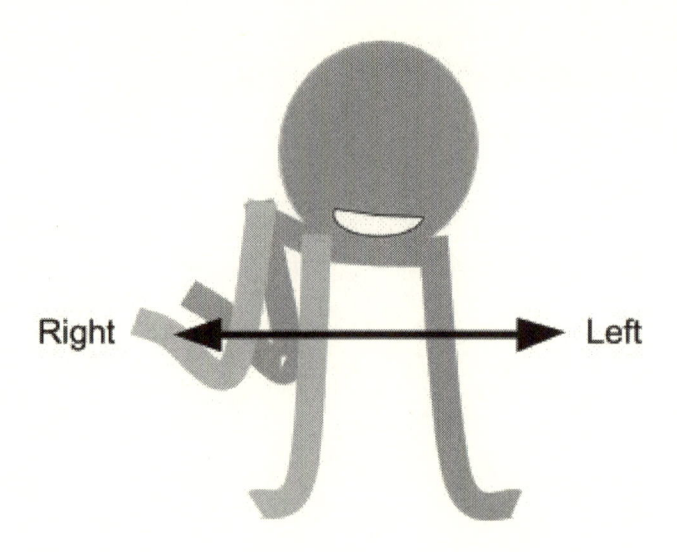

How much? How often? How long? This is entirely dependent on each child. A recommendation for Vestibular stimuli is absolutely best provided by a qualified Occupational Therapist who has evaluated your child. But if your child already swings, twirls, jumps, etc, then you probably do not need to impose this type of stimuli upon them. They are getting it on their own. See if you can slow them down and give them better rhythm for the calming effect. If your child avoids Vestibular stimuli, and you do not have access to a qualified Occupational Therapist, I'd recommend starting very slowly and watching for adverse reactions. For example, 15-20 seconds of unfamiliar imposed vestibular stimuli, with a 48-hour watch period. Note any unusual behaviors, moods, sleep, digestion, etc. If you see anything unusual, don't impose any more Vestibular stimuli until you have your child evaluated by a qualified Occupational Therapist. If you do not notice any adverse reactions, increase duration by 5-10 seconds every 48 hours, up to 2 minutes. Vestibular stimuli should **NEVER** be imposed on a child with a known seizure disorder without professional guidance from a qualified Occupational

Therapist. This can be used as a maintenance technique, but is not likely to be helpful during a Fight, Flight, Freeze event.

- **Spinning/twirling** is a *rotational* vestibular movement, *not linear*, and does **NOT** tend to have a calming effect on most individuals. It actually tends to be arousing if it doesn't cause nausea. However, for those individuals who have under-responding vestibular systems, spinning can be a helpful tool for them to be able to regulate and organize. I **NEVER** recommend that anyone impose spinning on a child as a therapeutic technique unless they truly understand what it is doing to their processing. But I almost never have a problem with a child spinning themselves if they've already demonstrated a tendency for it.

Inversion is another type of vestibular stimuli in which the head is positioned below the center of gravity. It can have a calming effect on many people. The center of gravity on most people is roughly behind their belly buttons.

1. **Hanging over the arm of the couch or chair**. Do not force this activity if they do not enjoy it.
   How much? How often? How long? For the child that enjoys this and does it on their own, there is little reason to limit what they enjoy. Be sure they aren't going to fall off and hurt themselves. It can be done anytime during the day. This is best used as a maintenance technique and would also be effective during a Fight, Flight, Freeze event.

2. **Sunrise Stretches**: have your child inhale as they reach over their head, then slowly reach down to touch their toes as they exhale. This would combine vestibular and proprioceptive sensory input, along with breath control.

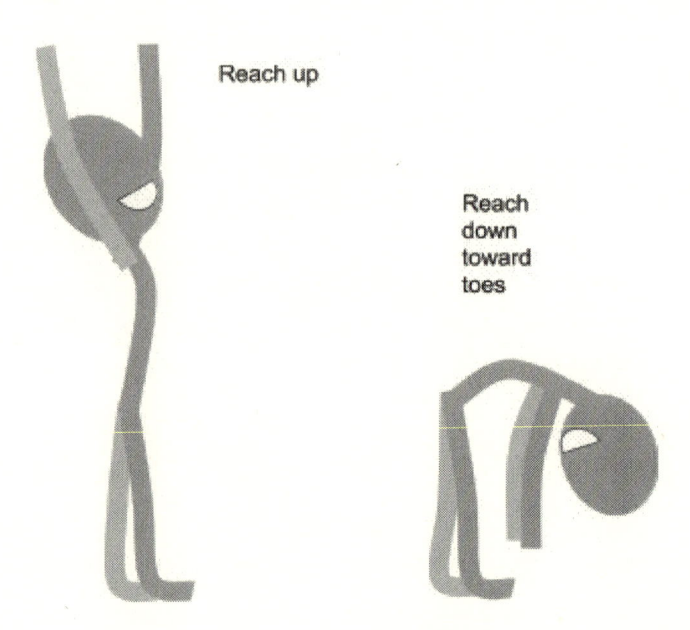

Reach up

Reach down toward toes

How much? How often? How long? Start with 5 repetitions and slowly build up to a maximum of 25 repetitions at one time. This is more beneficial if performed in the mornings, but can be done in the afternoon or evening. It may be somewhat alerting for some, and could interfere with sleep if done too close to bedtime. It's safe to do this daily, but 3-5 times a week would be sufficient. This is an activity that can be done throughout someone's lifetime. This is best used as a maintenance technique and would also be effective during a Fight, Flight, Freeze event.

3. **Laying On or Rolling** slowly over a therapy ball while on their belly will bring their head below their center of gravity, assuming that the ball is big enough. It could also provide repetitive linear vestibular

input if they rock back and forth, and if they land on their hands and feet with any pressure, it will provide proprioceptive input as well.

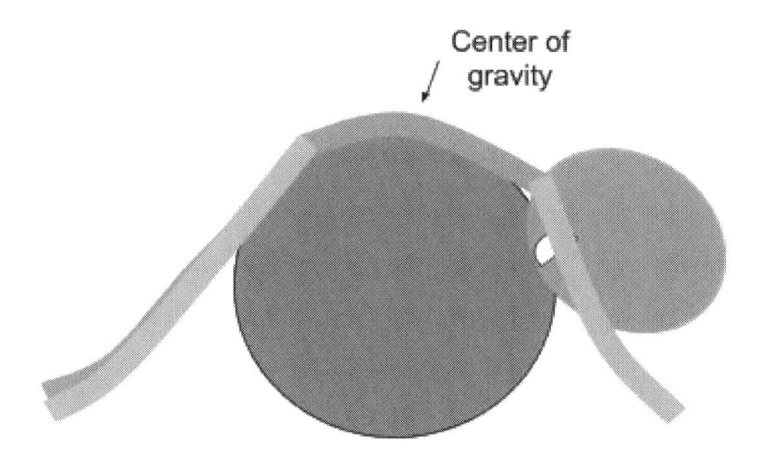

Center of gravity

How much? How often? How long? Start with 5 repetitions and slowly build up to a maximum of 20 repetitions at one time, 3-5 days a week.. However, for the child that enjoys this and does it on their own, there is little reason to limit what they enjoy. Be sure they aren't going to fall off and hurt themselves. It can be done anytime during the day. This is best used as a maintenance technique and would also be effective during a Fight, Flight, Freeze event.

4. <u>**Hanging upside down on the monkey bars**</u>, assuming you think it's a safe activity for them.
   How much? How often? How long? For the child that enjoys this and does it on their own, there is little reason to limit what they enjoy. Be sure they aren't going to fall off and hurt themselves. It can be done anytime during the day. This is best used as a maintenance technique and would not be effective during a Fight, Flight, Freeze event.

5. <u>**Headstand or Handstand**</u>, assuming you think it's a safe activity for them. This can be particularly helpful if they are in sports where this is performed, such as gymnastics.

How much? How often? How long? Again, this depends on each child. If your child is already doing this and not experiencing an adverse reaction, then it's probably fine to allow them to continue. If your child is *not* already doing this to calm and regulate, then you can introduce it by having them lay over a therapy ball and ease into it. Allow them to explore this technique to their tolerance and enjoyment. Do not force it. This can be used as a maintenance technique, but likely won't be effective during a Fight, Flight, Freeze event unless they are already seeking this input to self-regulate.

<u>Vibration or Bone Conduction</u> is another way to stimulate the Vestibular system.

1. **Humming/"Om"**. Humming provides bone conduction to our head and spine. (Try it. Place your hand lightly on your neck and hum. Do you feel the vibration? That just figuratively "shook your brain!") This vibration stimulates the vestibular receptors in our inner ears. This activity also provides slight proprioceptive input as well, so you have multi-sensory input working to calm and organize your child's brain. Have your child sing or hum their favorite song, the alphabet song, recite a prayer, or just hum. They may already do it themselves, and if so, it probably drives you nuts. Kids are smart and figure out what makes them feel better. And then we, as parents and professionals, try to take their coping mechanisms away and wonder why they aren't coping. Find a compromise that doesn't drive you nuts while they are trying to cope. Help them pick the song, wear ear plugs, or sing along!
How much? How often? How long? Limitations are based upon parental (and sibling/family) tolerance! This can be used as a maintenance technique, and during a Fight, Flight, Freeze event.

The Auditory System

Auditory is the sense of sound. The receptors are located in our inner ears. This processing does not refer to hearing ability or loss, though it could include that aspect. But rather, it refers to hearing processing. Is what the brain is understanding from the ears actually the sound that they are experiencing. Example, when you say "Go brush your teeth" does your child hear "Go brush her feet"? You may hear some professionals tell you that auditory processing cannot be changed, and the only option is to use compensatory strategies such as headphones, visual cues, and written instructions. There is actually evidence that auditory processing can indeed be changed, and we use many of the techniques in my office. But that is an aside. For now, let's look at a few ways we can calm our child via their auditory processing system.

1. **Music**. Let them listen to and/or sing their favorite music. (Remember, humming or singing provides bone conduction stimulating the vestibular system and the proprioceptive system at the same time, helping to calm and integrate.
   How much? How often? How long? Unlimited. This can be used as a maintenance technique, and during a Fight, Flight, Freeze event.

2. **Humming/"Om"**. humming provides auditory input as well as bone conduction to our head and spine. (Try it. Place your hand lightly on your neck and hum. Do you feel the vibration? That just figuratively "shook your brain!") This activity also provides slight proprioceptive input as well, so you have multi-sensory input working to calm and organize your child's brain. Have your child sing or hum their favorite song, the alphabet song, recite a prayer, or just hum. They may already do it themselves, and if so, it probably drives you nuts. Kids are smart and figure out what makes them feel better. And then we, as parents and professionals, try to take their coping mechanisms away and wonder why they aren't coping. Find a

compromise that doesn't drive you nuts while they are trying to cope. Help them pick the song, wear ear plugs, or sing along!

How much? How often? How long? Unlimited. This can be used as a maintenance technique, and during a Fight, Flight, Freeze event.

3. **Listening Therapies:** Listening Therapies typically involve the use of headphones and specially designed music that is intended to provide stimulation to an individual's brain in specific ways. Many of them have the added stimulation of bone conduction along with the air conduction (the music we hear). The music typically sounds normal to the listener. Most of the Listening Therapy programs are designed for the individual to listen to music while performing a variety of motor tasks, such as balancing on a balance board or playing catch. Some also offer different products to assist with more specific challenges, such as a pillow for better sleep.

   How much? How often? How long? Depends upon which Listening Therapy you are using. These are most often used as a maintenance technique, but not during a Fight, Flight, Freeze event.

The Visual System

Visual processing refers to the ability of the brain to perceive what the eyes are seeing. This does not necessarily refer to visual acuity, but that can be a component of visual processing. This *does* refer to such visual skills as Visual Discrimination, Visual Form Constancy, Visual Figure-Ground, Visual Memory, and more. Having a visual perceptual deficit, especially one that may be undiagnosed, can be extremely frustrating and tiring. And that would most definitely cause someone to have a shorter fuse for becoming frustrated, and to react to seemingly innocuous demands with what looks like an exaggerated reaction: fight, flight, or freeze. Let's look at what we can do to turn down the frustration and fatigue.

1. **Tinted glasses or filters:** Irlen Syndrome is a visual-perceptual processing disorder in which there is a sensitivity to light waves. This sensitivity can make many tasks challenging and result in a frustrated child who has a short fuse and may produce a Fight, Flight, Freeze response to tasks that are difficult due to the light sensitivity. Glasses that have been tinted to respond to an individual sensitivity are typically prescribed. Visit www.Irlen.com for more information. **How much? How often? How long?** Prescribed glasses are to be worn as needed and recommended by a specialist. This can be used as a maintenance technique, but not during a Fight, Flight, Freeze event.

2. **Color:** There is minimal and questionable research on the science of color and mood. However, anecdotally, many of us can recognize that some colors can elicit certain emotions. And they can often be identified by the adjectives that accompany the colors when we talk about them. For example: Green with envy. Singing the blues. Red hot. I personally use color in my environment to assist my mood regulation. There is little harm in providing items in a color that your child professes to like. For instance, if they want to wear lime green shoes to church because it's their favorite color, why not let them?

How much? How often? How long? Unlimited. This can be used as a maintenance technique, and during a Fight, Flight, Freeze event.

3. **Nature** visually stimulates in both alerting and in calming ways. Allow your child to explore the great outdoors, and stimulate not only his visual system, but his tactile/touch, his proprioceptive, his olfactory/smell, his auditory/hearing, and his vestibular/movement senses. Help him discover what helps him feel calm.
   How much? How often? How long? Unlimited. This can be used as a maintenance technique, and during a Fight, Flight, Freeze event with precautions for flight and risk of injury.

Calm Down, Child

Olfactory (Smell) and Gustatory (Taste) Sensory Systems

The sense of smell is closely associated with memories and emotion. For this reason, we can elicit emotions that are tied to memories just by presenting the aroma that goes along with that memory. Consider how the smell of fresh baked cookies affects you. Or the smell of fresh pines in the mountains, or salty air at the beach. You can use this association to help your child achieve a greater sense of calm.

The sense of taste can definitely be a rewarding sensory experience! Let's use this to our advantage, with moderation!

1. **Nature**: There are a variety of aromas in nature that can be calming. Flowers, salty air, pine in the mountains. Allow your child to explore the great outdoors, and stimulate not only his olfactory system, but his visual system, his tactile/touch, his proprioceptive, his auditory/hearing, and his vestibular/movement senses. Help him discover what helps him feel calm.
   How much? How often? How long? Unlimited. This can be used as a maintenance technique, and during a Fight, Flight, Freeze event with precautions for flight and risk of injury.

2. **Essential oils (EOs)** are readily available to most people these days. When your child is calm or sleeping, provide an essential oil for her to associate with that feeling. When she seems to feel anxious, re-introduce that oil to help her calm. There is a variety of essential oil jewelry available for both girls and boys, and allows them to access the aroma for a longer period of time. For example, an EO necklace

can be worn to school to help a child get through the day by providing that aroma all day long.

How much? How often? How long? To tolerances. This can be used as a

maintenance technique, and during a Fight, Flight, Freeze event.

3. **Foods** can be conduits to calm as well. The smell and taste of our favorite foods can often bring a smile to our faces. Of course, this should be used in moderation for the sake of your child's health.

    How much? How often? How long? Within a healthy diet. This can be used as a maintenance technique, but likely won't be effective during a Fight, Flight, Freeze event.

Interoceptive Sense

Interoception is the sensory system that lets you know what's going on inside your body. It alerts you to the sensations of hunger and thirst, to bowel and bladder urges, and to pain, illness, and itching. It also contributes to our emotional awareness and wellness. When this system is dysfunctional, a child may not realize that they are hungry or thirsty, or that a tooth hurts, or that they have to go to the bathroom until it's too late. As you can imagine, these mixed up signals about what's happening in our own bodies can be completely dysregulating and cause a sense of frustration and anxiety, laying the groundwork for even the smallest straw to break that camel's back and trigger a Fight, Flight, Freeze event. Below are some strategies to improve your child's interoception and ability to recognize how they feel, physically and emotionally, before they reach the point of Fight, Flight, Freeze.

1. **Body Mapping:** This refers to the practice of applying a light, but firm pressure to your child's body in order to "awaken" the receptors and provide increased tactile and proprioceptive stimuli to the brain to make it more aware. This is usually a pleasurable experience for the child. You, as the parent, provide the pressure by placing your palms on your child's belly, and tracing patterns on them. You can also utilize other items such as a soft dusting mitt, stuffed animal, toy car, etc. Many of these patterns are copyright protected like the one we use in my office. But there's one on Youtube called "Body Mapping Sam" that does a good job demonstrating it.
How much? How often? How long? 3 repetitions, twice a day, for up to 2 months. This can be used as a maintenance technique, and during a Fight, Flight, Freeze event.

2. **Wilbarger Brushing Protocol/Deep Pressure and Proprioceptive Technique (DPPT)**: This technique utilizes a surgical scrub brush (available on Amazon) to apply firm pressure to your child's body in a specific pattern to awaken the senses and provide the brain increased feedback for improved body awareness. This is a similar concept to

Body Mapping, and like Body Mapping, it is copyrighted. This technique is typically accompanied by joint compressions. I was trained in the Wilbarger Brushing protocol over 20 years ago, and have seen a variety of changes in the patterning and instructions. My general perception is that the point is to provide tactile and proprioceptive stimulation to the body simultaneously. The surgical scrub brush is a comfortable tool to use, and provides an easy visual to gauge the amount of pressure you are applying (bristles should be bent, not flat against the individual's skin). The pattern instructions depend upon who is teaching you and which pattern they themselves were taught. Again, you can look on Youtube.

How much? How often? How long? I was taught to provide this stimulation every 2 hours for 6 weeks. I feel like that is a huge mountain of homework to give most parents. If you can do 3 times a day for 6 weeks, that should help. This can be used as a maintenance technique, and during a Fight, Flight, Freeze event.

3. **Bowel/organ massage**: This is a simple way to do what I like to call "give a little tickle to your insides". It is an extremely light touch to the abdomen. Imagine a clock face on your child's abdomen, and starting at the right hip (around 8 o'clock) *very lightly* trace a circle on your child's abdomen in a clockwise direction. ***Lightly.***

   How much? How often? How long? As desired. If you see an undesirable change in bowel movements, STOP. This can be used as a maintenance technique, but likely won't be effective during a Fight, Flight, Freeze event.

4. **Zones of Regulation**: Here is another wonderful program to help your child become more aware of what their sensations are telling them about their arousal level, and their emotions. And again, it's copyrighted. I encourage you to Google it.

   How much? How often? How long? Depends on the activity you are using to teach the concepts. Not time consuming at all, but may be utilized for a long period of time until your child internalizes the concept. This can be used as a maintenance technique, but likely won't be effective during a Fight, Flight, Freeze event unless your child has internalized the concepts.

5. **Mindfulness Practices**: Out of all of the definitions I looked up for mindfulness, I like Wikipedia's the best. "Mindfulness is the psychological process of purposely bringing one's attention to experiences occurring in the present moment without judgment..." Here are some simple examples:

   a. <u>5-4-3-2-1 Method:</u> Name:
      - 5 things you can see (sky, cars, Mom/Dad, floor, etc.)
      - 4 things you can hear (clock, cars, TV, etc.)
      - 3 things you can feel (socks, underwear, tears on face, etc.)
      - 2 things you can smell (dinner cooking, vomit, perfume, flowers, etc.)
      - 1 thing you can taste (toothpaste, chicken nuggets, salt, etc.)

      How much? How often? How long? As much as needed. This can be used as a maintenance technique, especially to be familiar with the concept prior to a meltdown. It's best use will be during a Fight, Flight, Freeze event.

   b. <u>Describe an item.</u> Along the same lines, have something tangible in front of your child that they can see and touch. Ask them to describe it using their senses:
      i. What does it look like? Is it round, square, hard, blue, fuzzy, smooth, etc.
      ii. What does it sound like? Does it make any sound on its own? What about if you tap it?
      iii. What does it smell like?
      iv. What does it taste like (Or for something inedible, what do you imagine it would taste like?)

v. What does it feel like? Is it hard, soft, cold, rough, etc.?
vi. Finally, have them close their eyes and picture the item. Now ask, what could you do with the item? (Ex: if it's a ball, you could throw it, catch it, bounce it, etc. If it's a dog, you could pet it, hug it, walk with it, etc.)

How much? How often? How long? As much as needed. This can be used as a maintenance technique, especially to be familiar with the concept prior to a meltdown. It's best use will be during a Fight, Flight, Freeze event.

c. <u>**Blow out an imaginary candle.**</u> Have your child close their eyes and picture a candle, then blow through pursed lips like they're blowing it out.

How much? How often? How long? As much as needed. This can be used as a maintenance technique, especially to be familiar with the concept prior to a meltdown. It's best use will be during a Fight, Flight, Freeze event.

d. <u>**Yes, No, Maybe:**</u> Have the child gently nod their head "yes" 3 times, then gently shake it "no" 3 times, then gently rock ears to shoulders in a "maybe" 3 times.

How much? How often? How long? As much as needed. This can be used as a maintenance technique, especially to be familiar with the concept prior to a meltdown. It's best use will be during a Fight, Flight, Freeze event.

BEHAVIORAL

I do a Parent Workshop in my office titled "Creative Discipline" in which I discuss several behavioral techniques that I used as a mother, and that I continue to use as an Occupational Therapist. I didn't typically use rewards, nor did I typically use punishment. I attempted to teach and guide behavior before it ever got to a point that it needed to be corrected. And when it did get to that point, I still attempted to guide my children to choose the correct response, and then plan for a better behavior choice the next time they were in a similar situation. I take a similar approach with the children in my office as well.

1. **Have non-negotiables**. Make the rules very clear about certain behaviors. For example, hitting another person was never allowed in our house. If this occurred, the consequences were well spelled out in advance, and were carried out immediately. The rules for hitting someone in our house were to immediately apologize, whether you mean it or not, go to your room to cool down (for them, and often me!), and then there would be a discussion regarding what lead to the hitting. Once the whole story was out and the offending child was sufficiently aware of the error of their way, amends were to be made. Amends meant many different things, which I discuss in my Creative Discipline Workshops and (hopefully) future book.
How much? How often? How long? As the parent, you get to decide. This can be used as a maintenance technique, especially to be familiar with the concept prior to a meltdown. It will be difficult to enforce during a Fight, Flight, Freeze event, but will be necessary.

2. **Allow choices**. If a child tends to feel anxiety or frustration, those emotions will often elicit a fight, flight, or freeze response. As parents, we often perceive this response as disobedience and unintentionally make the situation worse by chastising them or punishing them. **If** we allow them choices in advance of triggering the fight, flight, or freeze response, we might just be able to avoid it.

But, WE must be the one determining the appropriate choices. Don't ask your child open-ended questions like "What do you want to do?" or "When do you want to eat?" YOU determine the appropriate options for your child to choose from first. It will feel like a lot more work on your part initially. But, if it helps us all avoid having to deal with a fight, flight, or freeze response, it will actually save us sweet time and energy in not having to deal with that. An example of a pre-determined choice would be, "Do you want to brush your teeth before you get dressed, or after?" Notice that this choice offered to the child makes the assumption that they *will* brush their teeth, and that they *will* get dressed. They are only getting to choose the *order* in which they get to do these tasks.

How much? How often? How long? As much as you can. This can be used as a maintenance technique, especially to be familiar with the concept prior to a meltdown. It will be difficult to utilize during a Fight, Flight, Freeze event, but might help ease a child out with desirable options. Be careful not to bribe your child to "come out" of the Fight, Flight, Freeze event. Respect that their response is based upon real feelings that they experienced, and must be processed.

3. **Role playing** allows an anxious child to practice what will *likely* happen in a certain situation, and to practice different options for their response in case "the worst" happens. I likely would have role-played better options for the example in #1 above if I had a child who had hit someone. We would have come up with several options for how to handle whatever the frustrating situation was that brought them to the point of hitting. Here's another example: if your child has a test coming up in school and they are anxious, role play what could happen:
    a. They could get 100% on the test. Do they jump up and down, boasting of their high score to the rest of the class or do they celebrate quietly in school, then come home and jump up and down with you?

    b. They could get a "B" and either be relieved, or disappointed that they didn't get an "A". How should they act in school? At home?
    c. They could fail the test. Again, role play how they should react in different environments with different people.
- We used role-playing for many different situations when my children were younger. One important one that I recommend that you practice is role playing for emergency situations. I used to role play that I had an "accident" in the house and fell down and couldn't get up. I taught my children to call 911 and provide correct information. Fortunately we never needed it, but it was good to know that they had been taught the emergency procedures.

How much? How often? How long? As much as you can. This can be used as a maintenance technique, but likely won't help during a Fight, Flight, Freeze event.

4. **<u>Catch your child doing something right or well</u>**. Praise them. Reward them Reinforce the behaviors you want to see more of. This requires you to be extremely vigilant to look for something that you may not already be attuned to. But I have faith that you can do it!
How much? How often? How long? All. The. Time. This can be used as a maintenance technique, but likely won't help during a Fight, Flight, Freeze event as it would be difficult to find something to praise. But if you can, do it!

PHYSIOLOGICAL

This refers to changing or influencing how the body functions.

1. **Medication**. You must go to a Medical Doctor (MD) or a Psychiatrist for medication. A Psychologist cannot write a prescription for medication.
   How much? How often? How long? Per Doctor's orders. This can be used as a maintenance technique, but likely won't help during a Fight, Flight, Freeze event.

2. **Epsom Salt Baths** are reportedly relaxing because of the many benefits of Epsom Salts. Epsom Salts aren't really salt at all, but rather are a magnesium sulfate. Folklore tells us that the magnesium gets absorbed by our skin and helps us calm. There is not sufficient clinical evidence to say definitively whether the human body absorbs Magnesium through our skin or not. But there is evidence that a warm bath, whether with Epsom Salt or bubbles or Bath Crystals, etc. can be relaxing. And there is no evidence that Epsom Salts are harmful. So go ahead and put some Epsom Salts in the bathtub and let your child soak!
   How much? How often? How long? Daily Epsom Salt baths are a comfortable routine. This can be used as a maintenance technique, but likely won't help during a Fight, Flight, Freeze event. But would likely be a good intervention after a Fight, Flight, Freeze event.

3. **Grounding mats** are intended to be a replacement for being able to actually get outside and neutralize the electrical charges in our body by being in contact with the earth. The practice of being barefoot outside to neutralize our electrical energy is called "Grounding" or "Earthing". Grounding mats typically have a single-prong plug that plugs into an outlet - but only in the ground-wire hole. This theoretically allows the electrical charges to conduct through the mat, the wire, the grounding plug, the ground-wire and into the earth. I

have 2 grounding mats and use them sometimes. I'm not sure of their actual benefit, but to my knowledge there is no harm in using them. I actually prefer to go outside barefoot and ground with the earth. Yes, I believe it makes a difference. I believe there is much benefit to be gained from touching the earth with our bare skin.
How much? How often? How long? Unlimited. This can be used as a maintenance technique, but likely won't help during a Fight, Flight, Freeze event.

4. **Herbs/supplements**: I am not an expert on this subject by a long shot. But I do take supplements intended to detox harmful substances and foods that I was sensitive to, and to assist my body in a healing process. I feel much better having reduced my systemic inflammation by both eliminating the foods and by taking the supplements. I recommend you seek out a nutritionist or a homeopath if you are interested in this technique.
How much? How often? How long? I am not qualified to answer this.

5. **Essential Oils (EOs)**: I briefly mentioned EOs above when talking about the Olfactory/Smell sensory system. EOs have been reported to have a multitude of benefits to the human body by both ingesting them and applying them topically. There is reliable research out there for much of it. I look at the use of EOs as a "personal preference" regarding which brands, which oils, which blends, and which application method. Keep in mind that some of them can be dangerous in certain doses or if applied in pure form.
How much? How often? How long? To tolerance. This can be used as a maintenance technique, and could be helpful during a Fight, Flight, Freeze event.

6. **CBD Oil**: CBD stands for Cannabidiol Oil, which comes from the cannabis plant, but is not marijuana. As of the writing of this book, federal law allows for the purchase of CBD oil as long as it doesn't

contain more than .3% of THC. The sticky part comes in with the regulation of growing and selling the oil. And each state has their own laws regulating it, or in some cases they don't have any laws regulating it...yet. In the Agriculture Improvement Act of 2018, the federal government legalized the availability of CBD for purchase by removing it from the Controlled Substances Act and placing it under the jurisdiction of the US Department of Agriculture. But the Food and Drug Administration have authority over the derivatives of the cannabis plant, and they are currently investigating the safety of CBD oil. Basically, there's a lot of gray area and the FDA and the states are scrambling to write the laws and regulations regarding CBD oil sales and purchases.

In the meantime, you can find the product available almost everywhere, and in many forms. And it has been helpful for many people. That's all I'm going to say about that until the laws are clearer.

How much? How often? How long? I am not qualified to answer this.

ALTERNATIVE

Alternative techniques are techniques that are not generally recognized by the healthcare professionals as "Evidence Based Practice" (EBP) and are not typically covered by health insurance. Most often, these techniques do have evidence to support their use, but not enough, and not strong enough for many in the healthcare professions to endorse or use them. That being said, I have used many of them on myself and my family. I'm also aware of many friends and clients utilizing techniques in this category with a variety of benefits. I encourage you to investigate them if you are interested.

1. **Acupuncture**: The Mayo Clinic describes Acupuncture as involving "the insertion of very thin needles through your skin at strategic points on your body. A key component of traditional Chinese medicine, acupuncture is most commonly used to treat pain. Increasingly, it is being used for overall wellness, including stress management."
How much? How often? How long? Per the professional advice and recommendations of a licensed acupuncturist.

2. **Acupressure:** According to WebMD, acupressure is described as "one of a number of Asian bodywork therapies (ABT) with roots in traditional Chinese medicine (TCM)" in which "Traditional Chinese medical theory describes special acupoints, or acupressure points, that lie along meridians, or channels, in your body. These are the same energy meridians and acupoints as those targeted with acupuncture. It is believed that through these invisible channels flows vital energy -- or a life force called qi (ch'i). It is also believed that these 12 major meridians connect specific organs or networks of organs, organizing a system of communication throughout your body. The meridians begin at your fingertips, connect to your brain, and then connect to an organ associated with a certain meridian. According to this theory, when one of these meridians is blocked or out of balance, illness can occur. Acupressure and acupuncture are among the types of TCM

that are thought to help restore balance. You can access your own acupressure points.

How much? How often? How long? As needed. This can be used as a maintenance technique, and could be helpful during the build-up to a Fight, Flight, Freeze event. I'm not sure how helpful it can be during a Fight, Flight, Freeze event.

3. <u>**Qigong**</u>: The National Qigong Association defines the practice as "a mind-body-spirit practice that improves one's mental and physical health by integrating posture, movement, breathing technique, self-massage, sound, and focused intent."

   How much? How often? How long? Per the professional advice and recommendations of a trained Qigong provider.

4. <u>**Cupping**</u>: According to Healthline, "Cupping is a type of alternative therapy that originated in China. It involves placing cups on the skin to create suction. The suction may facilitate healing with blood flow. Proponents also claim the suction helps facilitate the flow of "qi" in the body."

   How much? How often? How long? Per the professional advice and recommendations of a trained cupping provider.

5. <u>**Reiki**</u>: Reiki.org describes it as "a Japanese technique for stress reduction and relaxation that also promotes healing. It's administered by laying on hands…"

   How much? How often? How long? Per the professional advice and recommendations of a trained Reiki provider.

6. <u>**Tapping**</u>: The Tapping Solution describes tapping as "a combination of Ancient Chinese Acupressure and Modern Psychology that works to physically alter your brain, energy system and body all at once." We have utilized their books for children and teenagers in our office. This is a technique I use myself, and find it very beneficial.

How much? How often? How long? Can be done anytime, anywhere, for any duration. This can be used as a maintenance technique, and could be helpful during the build-up to a Fight, Flight, Freeze event. I'm not sure how helpful it can be during a Fight, Flight, Freeze event.

7. **Emotional Freedom Technique (EFT)**: Similar to Tapping. "Emotional freedom technique (EFT) is an alternative treatment for physical pain and emotional distress. It's also referred to as tapping or psychological acupressure." ~ Healthline
How much? How often? How long? Can be done anytime, anywhere, for any duration. This can be used as a maintenance technique, and could be helpful during the build-up to a Fight, Flight, Freeze event. I'm not sure how helpful it can be during a Fight, Flight, Freeze event.

8. **Thymus stimulation/thumps**: This is another technique we utilize in the office. "The Thymus Thump (also known as the happiness point) can assist to neutralize negative energy, exude calm, revamp energy, support healing and vibrant health, and boost your immune system. A simple but very effective energy technique involves tapping, thumping or scratching on the thymus point. The word thymus comes from the Greek word 'thymos' which means "life energy." The thymus gland lies just beneath the upper part of the breastbone in the middle of the chest. It is the controller of the body's Meridian system. Its role is in keeping your own life energy vibrating in high frequency. When the thymus gland is in harmony can increase your strength and vitality. Dr. John Diamond, author of "Life Energy" maintains the thymus gland monitors and regulates the body's energy flow." From Balanced Health Clinic.
How much? How often? How long? Can be done anytime, anywhere, for any duration. This can be used as a maintenance technique, and could be helpful during the build-up to, and during, a Fight, Flight, Freeze event.

9. **Meridians**: Meridians are often described as a system of channels or tubules that run throughout the human body, carrying "qi" (pronounced "chee") or life energy, and a variety of other substances. It has also been described as the Primo Vascular System, and in 2016, Auburn University published an article highlighting that one of their researchers had discovered a "microstructure of the miniscule, translucent system of vessels, subvessels and stem cell-filled nodes—together making up the primo-vascular system—running throughout a rat's body, appearing in and on blood vessels, organ tissue and the lymphatic system." (See References) Often people will refer to running meridians to clear the blockages. We do this in our office, very minimally, but have seen benefit.

    How much? How often? How long? Can be done anytime, anywhere, for any duration. This can be used as a maintenance technique, and could be helpful during the build-up to a Fight, Flight, Freeze event. I'm not sure how helpful it can be during a Fight, Flight, Freeze event.

10. **Salt lamps**: Himilayan Salt Lamps are decorative lights that are carved out of pink Himilayan salt. According to Healthline, they are natural ionizers, changing the electrical charge of the ambient air. However, there is no evidence that these salt lamps can remove impurities from the air, and they have extremely limited evidence of any other benefit besides being an attractive night light. That being said, they do not have any reported harmful benefits, and in my opinion they fall under the category of "won't hurt, might help". I have two of them. This can be used as a maintenance technique, but likely won't help during a Fight, Flight, Freeze event.

    How much? How often? How long? Can be done anytime, anywhere, for any duration. This can be used as a maintenance technique. I'm not sure how helpful it can be during a Fight, Flight, Freeze event.

11. **Chakras**: Chakra literally means "wheel". There are 7 of them and they are believed to be the main energy centers of the body; each one representing different qualities.
    How much? How often? How long? I don't have enough experience with this technique to give you a definitive answer.

12. **Emotional Stress Release (ESR)**: I originally heard of ESR in the Touch for Health program which is a widely used system of kinesiology. ESR identifies two points on our forehead, roughly above the center of our eyebrows. Touching them is supposed to activate reflexes called neuro-vascular points, and thereby bring more blood to the frontal lobes of the brain. There is not much scientific evidence for this technique, or Touch for Health/kinesiology in general. But if you think about it, many of us intuitively rest our forehead on our hands, or rub our forehead with our finger and thumb when we're stressed or when we're deep in thought. So maybe there's something to it. At the very least, I have not found any evidence that holding these two points on your forehead with your fingers or palms is harmful. So, I would say that this falls in the category of "won't hurt, might help". We offer a diagrammed handout to our clients in our office to use this when they get stressed. We typically recommend 30 seconds to 2 minutes of light touch. Many have reported that it is helpful to them.
    How much? How often? How long? Can be done anytime, anywhere, for any duration. This can be used as a maintenance technique, and could be helpful during the build-up to a Fight, Flight, Freeze event. I'm not sure how helpful it can be during a Fight, Flight, Freeze event.

Emotional Stress Release (ESR) neuro-vascular points.

NOTES:

NOTES:

RESOURCES/REFERENCES

Anxiety and depression in children: Get the facts
https://www.cdc.gov/childrensmentalhealth/features/anxiety-depression-children.html

Data and statistics on Children's Mental Health
https://www.cdc.gov/childrensmentalhealth/data.html

https://www.ncbi.nlm.nih.gov/pmc/articles/PMC4006178/

Prayer:
https://psychcentral.com/blog/spirituality-and-prayer-relieve-stress/
https://www.mayoclinic.org/healthy-lifestyle/stress-management/in-depth/stress-relief/art-20044464
https://www.psycharchives.org/bitstream/20.500.12034/1534/1/psyct.v5i2.18.pdf

Hydration:
https://www.usgs.gov/special-topic/water-science-school/science/water-you-water-and-human-body?qt-science_center_objects=0#qt-science_center_objects
https://www.hsph.harvard.edu/nutritionsource/healthy-drinks-full-story/
https://ntcutah.com/how-does-hydration-affect-your-brain/

Breath Control
https://www.psychologytoday.com/us/blog/the-athletes-way/201905/longer-exhalations-are-easy-way-hack-your-vagus-nerve
https://www.betterhealth.vic.gov.au/health/healthyliving/breathing-to-reduce-stress

Sensory
https://www.spdstar.org/basic/your-8-senses
https://youngyogamasters.com/
https://integratedlistening.com/

Digging in the Dirt
https://permaculture.com.au/why-gardening-makes-you-happy-and-cures-depression/
https://www.gardeningknowhow.com/garden-how-to/soil-fertilizers/antidepressant-microbes-soil.htm
https://www.drnorthrup.com/dirt-strenthens-immune-system-happier-healthier/

Power Posing
https://www.forbes.com/sites/kimelsesser/2018/04/03/power-posing-is-back-amy-cuddy-successfully-refutes-criticism/#787577d3b8ef

Color Psychology
https://www.verywellmind.com/color-psychology-2795824
https://www.smithsonianmag.com/smithsonian-institution/ask-smithsonian-how-do-colors-affect-our-moods-180957504/

Interoception
https://www.spdstar.org/basic/your-8-senses

Epsom Salt
https://www.webmd.com/a-to-z-guides/epsom-salt-bath#1
https://www.ncbi.nlm.nih.gov/pmc/articles/PMC5579607/

Grounding Mats
https://www.healthline.com/health/under-review-grounding-mats#1

Essential Oils
https://www.ncbi.nlm.nih.gov/pmc/articles/PMC3607906/

CBD Oil
https://www.healthline.com/nutrition/cbd-oil-benefits
https://www.pbs.org/newshour/science/is-cbd-legal-heres-what-you-need-to-know-according-to-science
https://plantpeople.co/cbd-legal-states/

Acupuncture
https://www.mayoclinic.org/tests-procedures/acupuncture/about/pac-20392763
http://ocm.auburn.edu/newsroom/news_articles/2016/12/auburn-scientist-discovers-microstructure-of-primo-vascular-system.php

Acupressure
https://www.webmd.com/balance/guide/acupressure-points-and-massage-treatment#1

Qigong
https://www.nqa.org/what-is-qigong-

Cupping
https://www.healthline.com/health/cupping-therapy

Reiki
https://www.reiki.org/

Tapping
https://www.thetappingsolution.com/blog/what-is-tapping/

Emotional Freedom Technique
https://www.healthline.com/health/eft-tapping

Thymus Thump
http://www.balancedhealthclinic.co.uk/articles/19-the-thymus-thump

Meridians/Primo Vascular System
http://ocm.auburn.edu/newsroom/news_articles/2016/12/auburn-scientist-discovers-microstructure-of-primo-vascular-system.php

Emotional Stress Release (ESR)
https://static1.squarespace.com/static/5826a5bc893fc0eadc5a431f/t/5aaa450d8165f53165530d87/1521108242227/ESR.pdf

Salt Lamps
https://www.healthline.com/nutrition/himalayan-salt-lamp-benefits

Chakras
https://www.mindbodygreen.com/0-91/The-7-Chakras-for-Beginners.html

ABOUT THE AUTHOR

Kim L. Hazelton, has been an Occupational Therapist for 25 years. She specializes in helping children with retained reflexes, sensory processing disorder, autism, anxiety, and learning differences primarily through sensory processing therapy. In her practice she has developed a unique and effective approach to helping the children and families she works with. So unique, in fact, that she has been called an "irregular OT", "not a normal OT", and the professional title she is most proud of, "The **FUN**ky OT". Step one in her unique approach is to calm the Sympathetic Nervous system's Fight, Flight, Freeze response. She utilizes a variety of approaches in addition to sensory processing, and she now shares many of those techniques with you.

Kim has been married to her high school sweetheart for over 30 years. Together they have weathered the storms of life and parenting. They are the proud parents of two beautiful, unique, kind, and independent young adults.

Made in the USA
Middletown, DE
30 January 2025